DATE DUE

DEMCO 38-297

The Land and People of

SCOTLAND

The Land and People of®
SCOTLAND

by James Meek

HarperCollins*Publishers*

To Adrienne, Carole, Christiane, and Laura

Country maps by Robert Romagnoli

On pages 28–29, "Canedolia" from *Poems of Thirty Years,* Carcanet
Press, © 1982. Used by permission of the author.

On pages 194–195, "The Bonnie Broukit Bairn," by Hugh MacDiarmid, is reprinted
with permission of Mrs. Valda Grieve and Martin Brian & O'Keeffe
Ltd. Publishers.

On page 210, "Letter from America," by Charles Reid and Craig Reid © 1987
Warner Bros. Music Ltd. All rights on behalf of Warner Bros. Music Ltd.
for the Western Hemisphere administered by WB Music Corp.
All Rights Reserved. Used by permission.

The Land and People of Scotland
Copyright © 1990 by James Meek
All rights reserved.
Printed in the United States of America.
For information address HarperCollins Children's Books,
a division of HarperCollins Publishers,
10 East 53rd Street, New York, N.Y. 10022

Library of Congress Cataloging-in-Publication Data
Meek, James.
    The land and people of Scotland.

    (Portraits of the nations series)
    Bibliography: p.
    Includes index.
    Summary: Introduces the history, geography, people,
culture, government, and economy of Scotland.
        1. Scotland—Juvenile literature. [1. Scotland]
I. Title   II. Series.
DA762.M444 1990   941.1   88-27215
ISBN 0-397-32332-8
ISBN 0-397-32333-6 (lib. bdg.)

10 9 8 7 6 5 4 3 2

Contents

THE WORLD

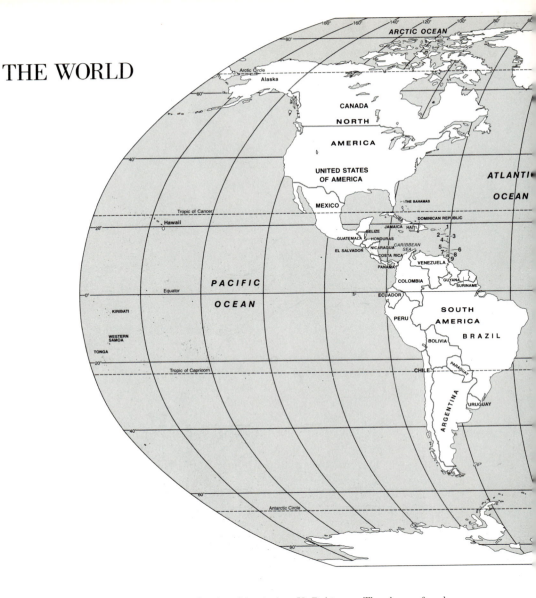

This world map is based on a projection developed by Arthur H. Robinson. The shape of each country and its size, relative to other countries, are more accurately expressed here than in previous maps. The map also gives equal importance to all of the continents, instead of placing North America at the center of the world. *Used by permission of the Foreign Policy Association.*

Legend

——— International boundaries

------- Disputed or undefined boundaries

Projection: Robinson

```
0        1000        2000        3000 Miles
0    1000    2000    3000 Kilometers
```

Caribbean Nations

1. Anguilla
2. St. Christopher and Nevis
3. Antigua and Barbuda
4. Dominica
5. St. Lucia
6. Barbados
7. St. Vincent
8. Grenada
9. Trinidad and Tobago

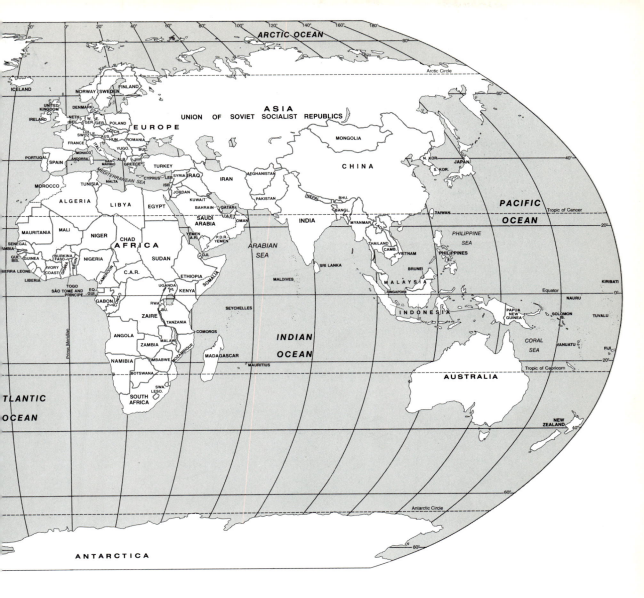

Abbreviations

ALB.	—Albania	C.A.R.	—Central African Republic	LEB.	—Lebanon	RWA.	—Rwanda
AUS.	—Austria	CZECH.	—Czechoslovakia	LESO.	—Lesotho	S. KOR.	—South Korea
BANGL.	—Bangladesh	DJI.	—Djibouti	LIE.	—Liechtenstein	SWA.	—Swaziland
BEL.	—Belgium	E.GER.	—East Germany	LUX.	—Luxemburg	SWITZ.	—Switzerland
BHU.	—Bhutan	EQ. GUI.	—Equatorial Guinea	NETH.	—Netherlands	U.A.E.	—United Arab Emirates
BU.	—Burundi	GUI. BIS.	—Guinea Bissau	N. KOR.	—North Korea	W. GER.	—West Germany
BUL.	—Bulgaria	HUN.	—Hungary	P.D.R.–YEMEN	—People's Democratic	YEMEN A.R.	—Yemen Arab Republic
CAMB.	—Cambodia	ISR.	—Israel		Republic of Yemen	YUGO.	—Yugoslavia

Mini Facts

OFFICIAL NAME: Kingdom of Scotland

LOCATION: Northwest Europe, the northernmost part of the British Isles. Its only land border is the 60-mile one with its southern neighbor, England. The Atlantic Ocean lies to the west and to the north, the North Sea to the east.

AREA: 30,414 square miles (78,772 square kilometers)—roughly between that of Maine and South Dakota

CAPITAL: Edinburgh

POPULATION: 5,117,000

MAJOR LANGUAGES: English. Scottish Gaelic is a significant second language.

RELIGIONS: Christianity (Protestant with a large Catholic minority)

TYPE OF GOVERNMENT: Participation in democratic monarchy

HEAD OF STATE: Hereditary queen or king of United Kingdom of Great Britain and Northern Ireland (UK)

HEAD OF GOVERNMENT: Prime Minister (of UK)

LEGISLATURE: The British Parliament. Scotland elects 71 of the 635 members of the House of Commons, Parliament's lower chamber. A variable number of unelected nobles—currently about 1,100—sits in the upper chamber, the House of Lords, of which a small proportion is nominally Scottish.

ADULT LITERACY: 99 percent

LIFE EXPECTANCY: Women, 75.5 years; men, 69.3 years

AVERAGE PER CAPITA INCOME: Approximately $9,400 (1987)

NATURAL PRODUCTS: Beef, beer, cereals, confectionery, dairy products, game, lamb, fish, soft fruit, tubers, timber, whisky, wool

INDUSTRIAL PRODUCTS: Aerospace equipment, bricks and cement, electronics, fertilizers, glass, heavy machinery, iron and steel, medical supplies, oil and gas exploration equipment, paper, petrochemicals, ships, textiles

SCOTLAND
CITIES AND REGIONS

0 10 20 30 40 50
MILES

ORKNEY

Kirkwall

SHETLAND

Lerwick

WESTERN ISLES

Stornoway

John O'Groats

Thurso

Wick

Ullapool

Lossiemouth

Fraserburgh

Dingwall

Nairn

Elgin

Banff

Peterhead

HIGHLAND

Inverness

Huntly

Inverurie

Portree

Kyle of Lochalsh

Aviemore

GRAMPIAN

Aberdeen

Braemar

Stonehaven

Mallaig

Fort William

Pitlochry

Forfar

Montrose

TAYSIDE

Blairgowrie

Dundee

Arbroath

Atlantic Ocean

Perth

St. Andrews

Oban

FIFE

15

North Sea

CENTRAL

Stirling

14

Kirkcaldy

Dunbar

1

2

11

12

13 **Edinburgh**

3 4 **Glasgow** 6 7

LOTHIAN

5

8

Berwick

Ardrossan

10 9 Lanark

Peebles

Galashiels

Irvine

Kilmarnock

STRATHCLYDE

BORDERS

Jedburgh

Ayr

Cumnock

Hawick

Campbeltown

Girvan

DUMFRIES & GALLOWAY

Dumfries

Lockerbie

ENGLAND

Annan

N. IRELAND

Stranraer

Wigtown

Kirkcudbright

Carlisle

Newcastle

Belfast

KEY TO NUMBERED CITIES

STRATHCLYDE
1. Helensburgh
2. Dumbarton
3. Greenock
4. Clydebank
5. Paisley
6. Cumbernauld
7. Coatbridge
8. Motherwell
9. E. Kilbride
10. Hamilton

CENTRAL
11. Falkirk
12. Grangemouth

LOTHIAN
13. Livingston

FIFE
14. Dunfermline
15. Glenrothes

Introduction

Finding Scotland on the map is easy. There it is, at the far edge of Europe, flung out from England toward the Arctic Ocean. But pinning it down as a country of five million individuals is harder; it does not seem to fit any usual category. Ruled by a government beyond its borders, Scotland has its own unique legal system. It has been part of a larger political entity for more than 250 years, yet it has a history of independence to rival that of many modern European republics. Its people are proud of their heritage, their languages and their culture, and are proud to call themselves Scots. Scotland may be less than a nation-state, but it is far more than a state of mind.

What is Scotland's political status? At its simplest, it is one of four units making up a single state called the United Kingdom of Great

BRITISH ISLES

UNITED KINGDOM

REP. OF IRELAND

Shetland
Islands

Orkney
Islands

*North
Sea*

*Atlantic
Ocean*

SCOTLAND

Edinburgh

Glasgow

N.
IRELAND

Irish Sea

Dublin

REP. OF
IRELAND

ENGLAND

WALES

London

English Channel

Britain and Northern Ireland (known as Britain, or the U.K., for short.) The other three units are England, Wales and Northern Ireland. Of the four, England has by far the largest population.

"English" and "British" do not mean the same thing, although they are often confused. "British" is a description correctly applied to all citizens of the U.K., and Scottish people are, technically, as British as the English are. But it was not always so. The idea of "Britain" is a relatively recent one, and tremendous differences remain between the two peoples.

Until 1603, Scotland and England had separate heads of state; and until 1707, they had separate governments, in Edinburgh and London. Now both countries are governed from London, which has become the British as well as the English capital. Because of its size, England dominates the elected assembly—Parliament—which forms Britain's administration. Whether Scotland will put up with this arrangement forever, or seek more self-government, is one of the topics to be dealt with in this book.

There is much natural beauty in Scotland. Half the country is covered by the mountainous wilderness of the Highlands. The long coastline and islands are a region in themselves, a region of gales, cliffs, clouds of seabirds, hardy fishermen. Yet Scotland is far from being a rural nation: Alongside the remote glens and oceans is another picture, of a sophisticated, technologically aware society, a land of electronics factories and nuclear power.

Scots should not complain too loudly if the world has a slightly distorted picture of their country. Scottish culture and ideas have been seeded more widely around the world than those of some larger nations. Most people living outside Scotland can call to mind a selection of images to represent it: the skirl of the bagpipes, perhaps; a tartan scarf; a chorus of "Auld Lang Syne"; the evocative names—Glenfiddich,

Macallan, Drambuie—on Scotch whisky bottles; the Loch Ness Monster. But these are only the most obvious emblems of a country striving for a more complete identity in the Europe of and in the world of the twenty-first century.

One of Scotland's most successful exports has always been its people, millions of whom have settled abroad. Often these restless, adventurous voyagers find they can see their country clearly as a whole only when they look at it from a distance. This is as true today as back in the nineteenth century, when the Scottish novelist Robert Louis Stevenson—the author of *Treasure Island*, destined to end his days in Samoa—wrote this:

Scotland is indefinable: It has no unity except upon the map. Two languages, many dialects, innumerable forms of piety, and countless local patriotisms and prejudices, part us from ourselves. . . . When I am at home, I feel a man from Glasgow to be something like a rival, a man from Barra to be more than half a foreigner. Yet let us meet in some far country, and . . . some ready-made affections join us on the instant.

This book aims to find out just what causes these "ready-made affections," and what Scots see when, from overseas, they cast their eyes back at their native land.

The Land

In the Beginning

Nothing affects the story of a country so much as where it lies among the continents and oceans of our planet. When Western recorded history begins, we find Scotland placed at the very edge of the ancient world. Many thousands of years ago, the Earth's climate changed, and Scotland emerged from beneath a thick carpet of ice to become the obscure northwestern corner of the great Eurasian landmass.

For early civilizations of Europe and North Africa, such as the ancient Egyptians, Greeks and Romans, the Mediterranean Sea was the heart of everything. Mediterranean Sea means "sea at the middle of the Earth." Scotland did not exist in their minds except as a bleak, inhospitable no-man's-land, incredibly remote. In those days, and for centuries afterward, people looked at places differently from the way we look at them today. Beautiful scenery and wild, romantic countryside was for

The Old Man of Hoy—a crumbling pillar of rock by the cliffs on the Orkney island of Hoy. Scottish Tourist Board

them just so many miles of avoiding bandits and wolves and seeking shelter from the weather.

What was this wilderness that appeared from under the retreating ice cap? Scotland lies in the northern part of the British Isles. Its only land border is with England. This border, which was not firmly fixed until a few centuries ago, runs southwest from the mouth of the River Tweed to an estuary called the Solway Firth. (Estuaries, the tidal mouths of large rivers, are known as "firths" in Scotland.) To the east of Scotland is the North Sea; beyond that, Norway, Denmark and the entrance to the Baltic. To the west lie thousands of miles of empty ocean—the cold, stormy Atlantic—with Canada on the other side. North are the Faroe Islands and the Arctic Circle. Apart from England, the nearest sizeable country to Scotland is Ireland, lying just 12 miles (19 kilometers) from the southwest coast. Scotland's isolation from all but these two close neighbors was to prove crucial in its history.

The land of Scotland is very old. Some of its rock has been in place for more than a billion years. But the landscape and coastline that exist today have been shaped by more recent events. During the last Ice Age, glaciers—rivers of ice—crawled powerfully down from the frozen peaks, scoring solid stone and shifting tons of rubble, flattening the V-shaped floors of mighty valleys and shifting enormous boulders from hillside to hillside, where they still sit, oddly out of place on otherwise smooth slopes.

Perhaps as long as ten thousand years ago, the last glacier disappeared. The land, relieved of the crushing weight, rose up and settled; the oceans, brimming with melted ice, had reached their present level. The volcanoes, like those that still lie in the middle of Scotland's capital city, were long extinct. Human migrants were about to populate a country whose rough outlines modern Scots would recognize.

North and South

The mainland of Scotland can be split very roughly into three parts. The southernmost part is hilly, rolling country, stretching from coast to coast in a broad band across the present-day regions of Dumfries and Galloway (in the west) and the Borders (in the east). Few of the peaks are higher than 2,000 feet (600 meters.) This area, prosperous if thinly populated farmland in modern times, provided both a buffer and a battleground for warring armies during the centuries of conflict with England.

The middle part of Scotland is called the Central Lowlands. Often known nowadays as the Central Belt, it is a relatively small area of flatter, more fertile land surrounding the three major firths of Clyde, Forth and Tay. Each one has a large city beside it today, and it is in this area that the bulk of Scotland's population now lives. Early settlers found it more hospitable—and easier to invade—than the hilly country that sandwiched it to the north and south. Travel was simpler, too. Not

SCOTLAND
PHYSICAL

LAND OVER 1000 FEET

LAND UNDER 1000 FEET

– – – HIGHLAND LINE

▲ MOUNTAIN

ORKNEY ISLANDS

SHETLAND ISLANDS

Pentland Firth

Cape Wrath

OUTER HEBRIDES

LEWIS

HARRIS

North Minch

Loch Broom

Dornoch Firth

Moray Firth

Spey

Don

Aberdeen

NORTH UIST

SOUTH UIST

SKYE

Loch Torridon

Loch Maree

NORTHWEST HIGHLANDS

Great Glen

Loch Ness

Monadhliath Mts.

Cairngorm Mts.

BEN MACDHUI

Dee

BARRA

INNER HEBRIDES

RHUM

Loch Moidart

COLL

GRAMPIAN HIGHLANDS

BEN NEVIS

Glen Coe

Rannoch Moor

Loch Tay

Tay

Sidlaw Hills

Dundee

Firth of Tay

North Sea

TIREE

MULL

IONA

Firth of Lorn

Loch Awe

Loch Fyne

Loch Lomond

The Trossachs

Earn

Ochil Hills

Loch Leven

Atlantic Ocean

JURA

KINTYRE

ARRAN

Firth of Clyde

Forth

Firth of Forth

Glasgow

Edinburgh

Lammermuir Hills

Clyde

Pentland Hills

Moorfoot Hills

Tweed

ISLAY

Mull of Kintyre

North Channel

SOUTHERN UPLANDS

Cheviot Hills

REP. OF IRELAND

NORTHERN IRELAND

Solway Firth

ENGLAND

only can many parts be reached by river, but this is the part of Scotland that narrows most between the North Sea and the Atlantic: The two coasts are barely 30 mi. (48 km.) apart at their closest point.

There was another reason why the Central Belt would become the focus of power, population and money in Scotland. Under the rich soil lay other riches—iron ore, lead and, most of all, coal. Alongside ancient volcanic relics—the sudden hill ranges that dot the region—manmade hills of slag called "bings," the debris of mining, have appeared.

North of the Central Belt are the immense mountain ranges and deep lochs (lakes) of the Highlands. The mountains are not high by world standards—the tallest, Ben Nevis, is just over 4,400 ft. (1300 m.)—but their steep, gaunt, treeless appearance is awe-inspiring and unique. Much of the area is as wild now as it has always been. The bare peaks stand on either side of bleak glens (valleys), the landscape pierced with countless waterfalls and burns (streams), punched with lochs of every size, blotched with soggy peat bogs, heather moors and areas of bracken, littered with gray boulders and scree (heaps of stones at the foot of a slope).

Awareness of the Highland–Lowland divide can aid understanding of the way Scotland developed. As in other countries, people in the mountainous region were able to hang on to a wilder, rougher, more tribal way of life, while their neighbors in the fertile plains around the firths developed separately into settled farmers and town dwellers used to roads, machines and written laws. The difference between Highlanders and Lowlanders was eventually settled, in theory at least—but in a tragic and often cruel way, as will be seen later.

Even today, the existence of an immense wilderness within two hours' drive of any of Scotland's major cities has an effect on its people. Part of the Scots' love for their homeland stems from a possessive pride in the beauty of this unspoiled country. At the same time the unchangeable harshness of the northern glens, and of much of the rest of the country, has perhaps contributed toward a Scots tendency for pessimism. The people of other parts of Europe, such as southern England, northern France and Holland, have been able to dominate and control their softer, richer lands more completely, making them more confident of their ability to conquer nature.

East and West

Up to now Scotland has been looked at in terms of north and south, but there is another equally important divide that becomes obvious from a glance at the map: Scotland's coastline has two totally different faces. In the east, looking out at the North Sea, the coast runs relatively smoothly. The land slopes down gradually to beaches of sand or pebble, to rock pools and expanses of dune, although occasionally there are cliffs, like those at St. Abb's Head, south of Dunbar. But always there is an expanse of gently undulating countryside on the approach to the shoreline.

In contrast, the west coast is riven with a crinkly fretwork of deep inlets, where the sea probes far inland, often to the very foot of the mountains. In these "sea-lochs," on a calm day, shallow salt water will lap gently at muddy shingle beaches at the foot of steep, treeless peaks, far from the open Atlantic—a gentler version of the Norwegian fjords.

There is another difference. The boundary between the eastern mainland and the sea is total. Nothing but waves and wind lie between the Scottish coast and Scandinavia. In the west, on the other hand, it might seem from the map that chunks of Scotland were flaking off and drifting out toward North America. Almost eight hundred islands speckle the ocean, from Arran at the mouth of the Clyde to tiny St. Kilda at the brink of the Atlantic deeps. Some, like Skye and Lewis, are big enough for landscapes of their own, complete with mountain ranges and brown peat moors. Others are simple lumps of rock with the barest layers of

The rolling farmland of the Southern Uplands, near Scotland's border with England, with the Eildon Hills in the background. Scottish Tourist Board

soil clinging to their crevices—Ailsa Craig, for example, a massive dome-shaped plug of granite that dominates the seascape off Girvan like the shell of a gigantic crab.

North of the mainland lie the two island groups of Shetland and Orkney, as close to Norway as they are to central Scotland. Orkney, the southernmost group, is the flatter and greener of the two, although the Orkney island of Hoy boasts Britain's highest vertical cliffs—1,140 ft. (347 m.) high. Both archipelagoes are virtually treeless.

Wind, Rain and the Warmth of Mexico

The Scots have a word *dreich*. If the English knew what it meant, they would certainly use it to sum up their image of their northern neighbors' weather: dreary, dismal, drizzly, misty, gray. English people have the same low opinion of the Scottish climate as the rest of the world has—quite unfairly—of Britain's.

Scotland lies as far north as Moscow, southern Sweden and the Gulf of Alaska, but for the most part seldom gets as cold in winter. The sea is to thank for this. Chilly as it might seem to hardy December bathers, you will never see ice floes in Scottish waters. This is due not to the native properties of the Scottish seabed but to another stretch of water thousands of miles away—the Gulf of Mexico. An ocean current called the Gulf Stream carries the warmth of Central America across the Atlantic and north past Scotland's west coast. By the time it gets there, there's very little warmth left, and Glasgow will never be New Orleans, but it does the job: Witness the incredible ornamental gardens created at Inverewe on the northwest coast, where subtropical plants flourish only 600 mi. (1000 km.) from the Arctic Circle.

So winters are seldom severe. Yes, the mountain peaks will turn white with snow, as early as October, and stay white for months; in sheltered hollows in ranges like the Cairngorms, tiny patches of snow stay frozen all year round. Yes, roads will be blocked, villages and towns cut off, and—occasionally—trains mislaid in drifts as fierce blizzards rage. Yes, parts of Scotland are frost free for only eight weeks a year. But the country never has to endure months on end of frost and snow-storms. In coastal regions—and that means a lot of the country—snow rarely lies for more than a few days before melting. Often the big cities get just one blizzard a year, sometimes not even that. Winter is an unpredictable mixture: brilliant, sparkling, blue-skied mornings of hard frost one week, rain and breezes of springlike mildness another.

The down side of such gentle winters is that summers rarely make the sidewalks sizzle. While it is not unknown for Scottish sunbathers to tan in their own backyards, it is equally possible for rain to fall on almost every day in, say, August. The Scots' idea of a hot summer's day is anything over 70 degrees Fahrenheit (21° centigrade): 90 degrees plus (32°C) is a freak heat wave. The key word is uncertainty in all seasons. Rain pelting down suddenly from a virtually cloudless sky is common, and hikers who challenge the mountains in August in jeans and a T-shirt do so at their peril. On the other hand, the farther north you go, the longer the summer days: Lerwick, the capital of Shetland, enjoys twenty-three hours of daylight each day in June, when the sun barely dips below the horizon before rising again. The single hour of dusk around midnight is known as the "Simmer Dim."

The west coast tends to get more rain than the east, but a disconcerting feature of summers by the North Sea is the mist, known by the Norwegian word *haar*, which can pour inland like smoke off the still-cold waters on warm, clear days. The hurricanes, typhoons and tornadoes of hotter parts of the world are unknown in Scotland, but the wind blows most days. Orkney, Shetland and the Western Isles, particularly the Outer Hebrides, can have over forty gales a year.

Wildlife

Woodlands

Very little of Scotland's original forest survives. In the south and west of the country are remnants of the old oak woods; elsewhere, groves of birch, beech, ash and alder can be found. An oak near Dunkeld is said to be the last survivor of Birnam Wood, immortalized by the English playwright William Shakespeare in his play *Macbeth.* (The fact that the battle he described actually took place more than a day's march away over the mountains does not deter tourists!)

The bulk of Scotland's woodland now consists of coniferous trees. Again, there are patches of the ancient Caledonian pine forest left. But most of the one fifteenth of the country's surface area covered with conifers has been planted during the past few decades. Some of these commercial plantations are in private hands; the rest are owned and run by an organization called the Forestry Commission.

The growth of commercial forests has dramatically altered parts of the Scottish landscape. Bare hillsides have been cut into by special plows, and once-treeless glens now play host to neat ranks of identical conifers—Scots pine, spruce, larch or Douglas fir.

Although commercial forestry has brought new jobs, and made Britain's timber and paper industries less dependent on foreign imports, not everyone is happy about it. To many people the new forests lack the character of natural woods, where trees of all ages and species are mixed. Some also believe the beauty of formerly treeless areas is being destroyed. The argument over where to plant, and how much, is particularly fierce in the northernmost part of the mainland, the district of Sutherland, where a huge area of bog known as the Flow Country is being steadily sliced into by private tree plots.

Some areas will never become forests. They are too wet, too steep, too rocky and, in particular, too windy. The west coast and the islands are battered by such fierce gales—gusting up to 126 mi. (200 km.) per hour—that trees can't survive. On the western mainland, few will be found growing above a thousand feet. Oddly, though, more sheltered regions of the same coast produce a completely opposite effect. The cool, moist climate is just what the bigger, imported North American pines like, and soon Scotland will have the tallest trees in Europe.

The wildlife of the Scots forest varies according to the age of the woodlands. The oldest woods are open havens for wild flowers, insects and birds; the most dense of the new plantations are silent, dark places where little sunlight penetrates to ground level and a brown carpet of pine needles muffles any sound.

Many birds nest in the forests. Woodpeckers, goldcrests and cross-bills roost among the universal blackbirds, wrens and chaffinches. Owls of three species—tawny, little and long-eared—hunt by night, sparrow hawks, kestrels and hen harriers by day. Nearer the ground stalk the game birds, pheasant, woodcock and capercaillie. This last is the biggest game bird in the British Isles. Weighing up to 12 pounds (5.5 kilograms), its name comes from the Gaelic *capull coille*, meaning "horse of the woods." It is famous for its strange mating calls and its habit of attacking animals much larger than itself, such as human beings. The capercaillie has made quite a comeback. Although it became extinct in Britain in the eighteenth century, breeding pairs brought over from Scandinavia 150 years ago flourished, and the bird's future seems secure.

Moor and Mountain

Looked at on the map, the Highland wilderness seems tiny compared to the deserts of Africa, the steppes of Russia or the American prairie; and in terms of square miles, it is. But there are many, many glens where the walker can stand on a bare slope and see no roads, buildings or living creatures in any direction. Sometimes the silence—broken only by the cry of a bird or the sudden roar of a jet fighter practicing low-level flying—can seem oppressive. Depending on the observer's mood and the state of the ever-changing weather, the scenery can be frighteningly bleak or upliftingly beautiful. There are few sights more magnificent than the sudden discovery of a hidden loch, thousands of feet above the floor of the glen, caught in an ancient fold of granite, deep and blue and icy cold. There can be few places more lonely than Rannoch Moor at dusk on a drizzly day, with the expanse of bog and dark pools and ochre grass stretching off into the murk.

The Highlands is, of course, no desert, and to describe it as a wilderness is not strictly accurate. Empty as it seems, the acres of unfarmed land are looked after. Sheep graze everywhere, and landowners control the number of deer and game birds on their territory to provide targets for fee-paying tourists' shooting parties.

Large expanses of bare rock are rare in the mountains. More commonly the slopes are covered in a thick, springy carpet of heather, dull brown except when it flowers, turning the glens a glorious purple color. Mixed in with this are areas of tough grass or bracken. Elsewhere the ground is wetter and breaks up into reed tussocks and spongy moss. The most difficult territory for the walker is the peat bog, where deep depressions pit the landscape, their floors a deceptively firm-looking layer of black. (Peat looks like a cross between loam and soggy coal.)

In spring the patchwork of heather, grass and bracken is lightened by a host of arctic and alpine flowers. In autumn tiny bittersweet "blaeberries" can be found on the higher slopes. But on most moors and mountains the constant nibbling of sheep, deer and birds makes

A ptarmigan, bird of the high peaks, in autumn plumage. John Marchington/Royal Society for the Protection of Birds

sure no more substantial shrubs or trees get a chance to grow. The regular heather burning by landowners, to allow tender shoots of vegetation to sprout for sheep, also limits the variety of plant life.

The game bird of the Highland moors and lower slopes is the red grouse, which often startles hikers by exploding from the heather at their feet, not wishing to abandon its hiding place until the last minute. For eight months of the year it is left alone; then, on August 12—the "Glorious Twelfth"—the official shooting season begins. A curious custom has grown up involving a race to see who can get the season's first grouse from the moors to someone's dining table. People have used helicopters, motorcycles, and even parachutes in recent years.

Farther up the mountain, the ptarmigan (the "p" is silent) is the hunters' target. An arctic bird, it is well adapted to the harsh conditions of the high peaks. It changes its plumage three times a year. In summer it is gray and white, blending in among the stones and lichen. It sits out the snows of winter in feathers of pure white, and wears an in-between shade in autumn. Like the ptarmigan, the mountain hare— very similar to its Lowland cousin in summer—changes its coat to a white one with the coming of the first frosts.

What predators do these creatures fear? Apart from people, there are three: foxes, wildcats and golden eagles. The second of these is one of the few species of wildcat in Europe. It hunts mainly by night, and is seldom seen. Snoozing on a rock in daytime, it might look like a rather muscular domestic tabby, but see it spit and snarl and there is no doubt that a saucer of milk is the last thing on its mind.

The golden eagle is the bird that more than any other creature conjures up the wild spirit of the remotest Scottish mountains. Soaring lazily above the moors, it can see for miles and carry off prey as large as young deer in its powerful talons. Because it needs an undisturbed rock ledge to build an eyrie, and because it needs an immense territory

A wildcat shows its teeth.   Dennis Avon/Ardea London

to hunt in, there are less than two hundred pairs in Scotland. Farmers who try to poison them because they occasionally kill lambs do not help, but for the time being at least, the eagle survives.

Red deer roam the Highlands in large numbers. Sometimes a herd more than a hundred strong will appear on the skyline, the antlers of stags making them look from a distance like some tribe of spear-carrying warriors. Smaller than their ancestors or their European cousins thanks to a poorer diet, they, like the grouse and ptarmigan, are controlled in order to be shot for sport. Recently, however, efforts have been made to farm them for their meat.

A golden eagle, largest bird in the British Isles, watches over its young in its mountain eyrie. C. Palmer/The Royal Society for the Protection of Birds

Rivers and Lochs

Fresh water is everywhere in Scotland, in every form: from the thousands of tiny mountain burns and waterfalls to the 118-mile-long (190 km.) River Tay, from puddles in peat scoops to Loch Lomond, at over 27 square miles (70 sq. km.) the country's largest body of inland water.

Few of the fast-flowing rivers, gushing down rocky pathways toward the sea, are polluted. Their purity is a boon to thirsty climbers, to whisky manufacturers and, of course, to fish. Trout, pike, perch, roach and lamprey are all found in the middle and lower reaches. But the prince of the rivers, the target for eager anglers and poachers, is the salmon. This sought-after fish is common in many of the larger rivers, particularly in the Tay, although every few years there is a scare that something—disease, poaching, overfishing—is seriously reducing its numbers.

A river gushes down from the mountains of Galloway, in the southwest of Scotland.
Author

Each year the salmon make a grueling journey upstream to lay their eggs in ancient spawning grounds. To do this they have to battle against ferocious currents and must literally leap out of the water to climb waterfalls. Since scientists learned how to generate power from the force of falling water, however, a host of hydroelectric projects has forced designers to dream up ways for salmon to get past high dams. At Pitlochry, engineers have built a "fish ladder": The salmon climb 60 vertical feet (18 m.) via a 340-yard-long (311 m.) chain of pools and underground pipes. Visitors can watch the fish swim past at a glass-walled observation point. At Loch Awe, salmon enjoy the ultimate luxury: an electric elevator.

The fish in Scotland's thousands of lochs are much the same as those of the rivers. Trout in particular are plentiful, and foreign varieties have been introduced to spice the hauls of anglers.

An increasingly common sight in sheltered inlets in both sea and freshwater lochs is the wire cage of a fish farm, where fish such as salmon are raised in captivity. Unlike those of countries like Japan, Scottish fish farms are relatively new—a solution to high unemployment in the Highlands—and as with the growth of forestry, some conservationists fear they are yet another step toward the destruction of the wilderness.

The ancient convulsions of Scotland's rocks produced many folds and faults, and some lochs are surprisingly deep. The deepest, Loch Morar, goes down as far as 1,077 ft. (330 m.). No one knows exactly what creatures live in the dark, cold world of these uttermost depths. Some fish that are known to inhabit such places—the char, for example, and the vendace, which may be unique to Scotland—are almost certainly stranded relics of an age when the seas were much higher than they are today.

Gaelic legend speaks of an animal called the *Each Uisge* (pronounced "ayukh ooshkuh"), meaning "water horse," and accounts of a monstrous beast living in long, deep Loch Ness date back many centuries. The Loch Ness Monster has been seen by more people than Bigfoot and photographed more convincingly than the Abominable Snowman. The best eyewitness account dates from 1933, when an English tourist couple claimed it crossed the road in front of their car. Later they wrote:

It was a loathsome sight. It seems futile to describe it because it was like nothing I had ever read about or seen. It was terrible. Its colour, so far as the body was concerned, could be called a dark elephant gray. It looked like a huge snail with a long neck.

However, despite costly expeditions involving round-the-clock watches, underwater cameras and sonar, no one has ever proved the monster's existence, let alone caught one. Most scientists remain skeptical, putting sightings, pictures and films down to explanations like otters, seals, logs or unusual waves.

The Coast, the Islands and the Sea

There may be adults in Scotland who have never seen the ocean, but it is doubtful. Everyone lives within easy reach of the Atlantic or the North Sea—usually both. Counting every island, the Scottish coastline stretches for 6,375 mi. (10,255 km.).

The shoreline is very varied. In a single 25-mi. (40 km.) stretch on the east coast between Dundee and Montrose, one can find the soft sand dunes of Buddon Ness, the red sandstone cliffs of Arbroath and the rock pools of Easthaven. Some of the most beautiful sand beaches, like Tentsmuir in Fife and Sandwood Bay in the far northwest, cover many acres and can be completely deserted, even in high summer.

Scotland is a key location for migrating birds, a crucial winter base for geese and ducks that have spent summer north of the Arctic Circle. As the geese arrive, seabirds like the gannet are flying south from

An unusual shot of a puffin in flight. Thousands of puffins nest in burrows above Scotland's seacliffs. David Urry/Ardea London

Scotland for warmer climes. The gannet is the biggest of the country's seabirds, with a wingspan that can reach 6 ft. (2 m.). It lives in massive "gannetries." One of the world's biggest gannetries is on Ailsa Craig, where more than fourteen thousand pairs are thought to nest together.

That odd bird the puffin is fond of Scotland too; 55,000 pairs breed in Orkney alone (they are known there as *tammie norries*). They nest in burrows in the ground and have an endearing habit of arranging the little silver fish they catch in neat rows in their brightly colored, spade-shaped beaks. Guillemots, kittiwakes, razorbills, fulmars, skuas and terns also nest in great numbers on cliffs and islands around the coast.

Two species of seal, the gray and the common, live in Scottish waters. Thriving despite a sometimes uneasy relationship with fishermen, they usually breed on remote islands and deserted stretches of coast, but can be seen at much closer quarters. One colony lives in the harbor at Stornoway, capital of the Western Isles; another frequents the sandbanks around the Tay bridges opposite Dundee.

Fishermen reap a rich harvest from the seas around Scotland, although the pattern of commercial fishing has altered drastically over the past few decades. Lobsters, crabs, prawns and shrimps are plentiful.

Herring, once the mainstay of Scottish fishing, has been overfished since the Second World War, and despite a ban on catching it between 1978 and 1981, its numbers have not recovered. Trawlermen are now more dependent on the mackerel. Cod, haddock, and whiting complete the bulk of the Scots catch.

Other inhabitants of the Scottish seas are halibut, skate—a weird diamond-shaped fish that can weigh up to 200 lb. (90 kg.)—and porpoise. Various types of flatfish, shark and whale are occasionally encountered in shallow inshore waters.

Oil and Gas

In 1964, the isolated Shetland bay of Sullom Voe was a virtually deserted backwater. Local people had little idea that hundreds of miles away the first hints were emerging of an immense treasure trove of oil and gas buried under the bed of the North Sea.

A generation later, Sullom Voe is the site of Europe's biggest oil terminal, processing more crude oil than the entire output of Iraq or Libya. To the wry Scots who had looked on the beauty of the Highlands and remarked, "You can't eat the scenery," it must have seemed that a freak of nature millions of years ago had produced a genuine bonanza. But one day the oil will run dry. It may be after all that Scotland's most valuable natural resources are its rugged beauty, its rugged climate—and its people.

Wild Goose Place

The time: dawn, early October. The place: Caerlaverock salt marshes, on the Solway Firth just south of Dumfries. Wildfowl Trust Manager John Doherty puts down his binoculars and smiles in satisfaction as the first wave of more than ten thousand barnacle geese touch down, exhausted after their 1,600-mi. (2500-km.) journey from the Arctic isle of Spitzbergen.

In ancient times the Scots, ignorant of the birds' spring-summer breeding cycle far to the north, believed barnacle geese grew as fruit from the branches of a mythical tree. Nowadays they know about their incredible voyage, and know virtually all the Spitzbergen geese depend on Caerlaverock for their winter feeding.

Until the area was made a nature reserve in 1957, the birds' future looked bleak. Immediately after the Second World War only five hundred geese survived. Now they prosper. When, as sometimes happens, the entire population descends on the previously quiet marsh in a single day, it is an awesome sight.

Split between the British government's Nature Conservancy Council and the Wildfowl Trust—a private charity—the Caerlaverock reserve is a conservation success story. While protecting the geese and other rare creatures like the natterjack toad, it strives not to clash with farmers and huntsmen, and is designed to give visitors every chance to see wildlife at close quarters.

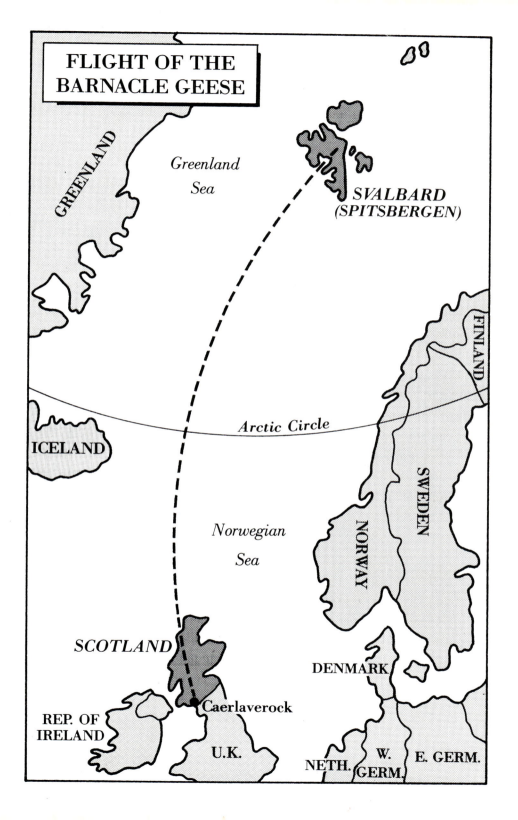

Scottish People, Scottish Tongues

Naming Scotland

There is another kind of geography than physical geography, a kind that you hear and speak rather than see: the geography of names. This is the geography that populates an otherwise barren map. And in the rich poetry of Scottish place names, the layers of ancient people and their languages stand out clearly. It is no exaggeration to speak of poetry. In the poem "Canedolia," by modern Glaswegian poet Edwin Morgan, an imaginary stranger asks about Scotland, and receives only place names in reply. "How far?" asks the stranger, and the answer comes:

from largo to lunga from joppa to skibo from ratho to shona from ulva to minto from tinto to tolsta from soutra to marsco from braco to barra from alva

to stobo from fogo to fada from gigha to gogo from kelso to stroma from hirta
to spango . . .
. . . what do you do?
we foindle and fungle, we bonkle and meigle and maxpoffle. we scotstarvit,
armit, wormit, and even whifflet. we play at crosstobs, leuchars, gorbals, and
finfan. we scavaig, and there's aye a bit of tilquhilly. if it's wet, treshnish and
mishnish.

All these are actual places, and the poem goes on to name such evocative
points on the map as Wamphray, Blinkbonny, Scrishven and Cambus-
puttock.

The ingredients in the modern Scottish mix of peoples are diverse.
Working back through time immigrants include Asians from former
British colonies; Poles and Italians fleeing poverty or oppression in
Europe; much earlier, French-speaking Normans; Vikings from Scan-
dinavia; Anglo-Saxons—the original English; Scots from Ireland; and
Picts who fought the Romans in the first century A.D.

The Picts left their mark in many place names, particularly in the east
of the country. Names beginning with *Pit* (Pitlochry, Pitsligo, Pitten-
weem) referred to Pictish farms. Those starting with *Aber* (Aberdeen,
Abernethy, Aberfeldy) spoke of the place where two rivers met or a river
met the sea.

Other names speak of the claims staked by the Gaelic-speaking Scots.
They replaced *Aber* with *Inver*, giving us Inverness, Inverkeithing and
Inverurie, and introduced the prefix *Kin*, meaning the head or top of
something—hence Kinross and Kinlochewe. The place name Kincar-
dine is testimony to the union of Picts and Scots: The Gaelic *Kin* is
joined to the Pictish *Carden*, meaning thicket. There are six different
Kincardines in Scotland.

Later, the Anglo-Saxons christened homesteads, which grew into
towns like Haddington and Coldingham, while the Norsemen gave

names to a host of settlements, particularly in the far north. The extreme north of the Scottish mainland is given the apparently upside-down name Sutherland (Southland) because it was the southernmost province of a Norse kingdom. Some of these Scandinavian names repeat themselves, changing slightly from place to place as they echo the far corners of the vanished Viking empire: Tinwald near Dumfries, Dingwall on the Cromarty Firth, Tingwall (one each in Orkney and Shetland) and Thingvellir in Iceland are all based on the same Norse root name, meaning an open-air parliament.

The final phase of naming came with the spread of English as the main tongue of Scotland. Market towns were called "burghs" (pronounced "burra"). Some had the word included in their name, like the English boroughs: Edinburgh, Musselburgh, Jedburgh. Meanwhile, aside from human settlements, the main features of the landscape—mountains, glens, rivers—kept and still keep their Gaelic names. These two languages, English and Gaelic, are what native Scots speak today.

Scots and the English Language

One of the strongest claims a people can make to nationhood is that they have their own language. It has been said that a nation is a dialect with its own army. For a people whose political independence exists only in the past, a unique tongue used among themselves is both a cultural safe deposit box for the present and a potential rallying point for the future. Scotland is unlike other countries in this respect, since English, its present first language, is the native tongue of numerous other states around the world.

But Scots are right to seek assurance of their separate identity in their language, for Scottish English is unique, and very different from the English of England, America or Australia.

Scots for Beginners

Key differences between Scottish and some American pronunciations of English are:

• Scots pronounce words starting with *wh* differently from words starting with *w*. In words like "what," "why," "where," they blow slightly after the *w* sound to represent the sound of the h.

• Scots often swap a double or single *t* in the middle of or at the end of a word for something called a "glottal stop." Instead of the t, there is a silent catch in the throat—like making an instant of silence into an extra letter. Try saying "butter" as if it were two words, "buh," "er," and you'll get the idea.

• Certain *oo* sounds—in "you," for example—are pronounced with the lips drawn more closely together than the American accent allows. Just make the usual *oo* sound, then gradually narrow the gap between your lips and make your lower lip jut slightly forward.

• Many Scottish place names have *ch* in them. This sound has no equivalent in American English, but think of a phrase such as "knock hard"; if you say the words together quickly enough the final *k* of "knock" and the initial *h* of "hard" will come together to make something like the Scottish *ch*.

• Unlike the long American *r* sound, with the tongue drawn well back, Scots trill the tip of the tongue against the palate to create the famous "rolling r."

There are two ways that varieties of the same language can differ. The first is in pronunciation: What kind of accent does a person have? The other is in dialect. What words, and what ways of forming sentences, are unlike those of other English speakers?

Scottish English and the English of England developed from the same medieval mixture of Anglo-Saxon and Norman French. Scottish English was well on the way to becoming a separate, standard form of speech—as different from that spoken in London as modern Norwegian is from modern Danish—when a dramatic political and religious upheaval swung it back into line with London English.

There is no such thing taught in Scotland's schools as a "correct" Scottish way of speaking or spelling. Scottish speech and writing are not taught at all. On the one hand, most modern Scots have the desire and instinct to use at least some Scottish vocabulary and grammar. On the other hand, the TV, radio, movies and books from England and America tell them that to do so marks them as unfashionable or socially inferior.

Most native Scots retain a distinct accent. Although there are common elements, accents differ widely from region to region. The amount of dialect vocabulary and grammar used also varies according to upbringing. The wealthy, people who went to college and people in white-collar jobs tend to use English that is closer to that spoken in London.

Some Scottish words and expressions are used and understood across virtually the whole country. Among them are: dinnae, cannae, willnae (don't, can't, won't), wee (small), aye (yes), ken (know), greet (weep), kirk (church), breeks (pants), lassie (girl), bairn (child), flit (move from one home to another), bonny (pretty), chap (knock), and bide (stay).

Other phrases, though using internationally recognizable English words, reveal their Scottishness not just by accent but by grammar.

Scots, for example, will say "Are you not going?" or "Are you no going?" rather than "Aren't you going?" And "I'm away to my bed," often replaces "I'm going to bed."

Beyond these well-used everyday words and expressions, every Scot has his or her extra Scottish vocabulary. In its heyday, the Scots tongue produced enough unique words to fill dictionaries as hefty as any Webster's, and many of these terms survive in one way or another. Scottish writers dip into the pool at will, enriching their English, often finding words for which there are no equivalents in any other language. *Gloaming*, for instance, means more than just "sunset"; it implies the whole light and atmosphere that envelops a landscape as the sun goes down. The speech of most older Scots is scattered with a selection of such expressions, and varying in degree from family to family, the younger generation follows suit.

There is a haphazard uncertainty about this passing-on process, which makes for awkward gaps in communication not just between the generations but in other relationships. Examples: A Scotswoman comes home from work one day and says, "I'm absolutely wabbit." Her friend will probably know *wabbit* means "exhausted," but may never have used the word before. A retiree complains to a young veterinarian about her cat: "He just sits there a' day, spanning his thrums." A perfectly normal way of saying "purring" to the elderly lady, but the veterinarian—who has lived in Scotland all his life—doesn't know what it means. A Scots schoolboy reads the first line of a poem: "She canna thole her dreams." He has never heard anybody use the Scots word *thole*, meaning "endure," and has to ask the teacher about it.

These daily crises in the survival of Scottish English are partly compensated for by the variety of dialect words and phrases that survive in the regions. Glaswegians, for instance, call children *weans*, not *bairns*. People in the northeast say *quine* instead of *lassie* for "girl," and replace "how" and "what" with *fa* and *fit*. Dundonians, as the inhabitants of Dundee are called, don't say *aye* for "yes," but *eh*. Dundee is the city where the glottal stop is taken to its greatest extreme, with the sentence "Yes, eat it all" emerging as "Eh, ee' i' a'." Orkney and Shetland have a deep wellspring of dialect words from their Norse past: *Faans* is what Shetlanders call a snowdrift; *haaf-fish* and *tang-fish* are Orcadian for the two different species of seal that frequent their islands.

Until very recently, the use of the Scots language in public life and in school was frowned on. Ever since Scotland was joined to England, efforts have been made by well-intentioned teachers and pro-London writers to make Scottish speech conform more to the southern pattern. But in the past fifteen years a resurgence of nationalist feeling and a growing respect for writers who use Scots of any kind in their work has given Scottish English a fighting chance. Joy Hendry said in 1985, hailing the publication of a new *Concise Scots Dictionary*:

Today, the position of the language couldn't be much worse in many ways, with fewer and fewer people actually speaking it in any reasonably pure form. . . . Yet survive it does. . . . Like predictions of the apocalypse, forecasts of the demise of Scots in X years have proved false; the beast refuses to die, though weakened by the blood-letting of centuries. . . .

Gaelic

The future of Scottish English depends on the degree to which Scots go on using their version of an international language. The future of Gaelic, Scotland's second language, depends purely on whether people speak it or not. It is a completely separate tongue, with its unique vocabulary and grammar, as different from English as are Greek or Polish. But it is in trouble. What was a thousand years ago the speech of Scotland's kings has now dwindled to the extent that less than 2

A typical crofting village on the Isle of Lewis. Here the everyday language would be Gaelic.   Author

percent of the nation's inhabitants speak it.

The stronghold of Scottish Gaelic—which is closely related to, but quite distinct from, Irish Gaelic—is in the northwest Highlands and in the Western Isles, although large numbers of native speakers live in the Central Belt, especially in Glasgow (over ten thousand). The highest concentration of all occurs on the island of Lewis in the Outer Hebrides. The largest town there, Stornoway, is the base for the civic authority, the Western Isles Council (*Comhairle nan Eilean* in Gaelic) and the true capital of the Scottish Gaelic-speaking world. Stornoway is the only town where you are likely to hear the language spoken regularly in the street. But even in the rural hinterland, one person in ten has no fluency in it.

Gaelic (pronounced "Gallic" by English-speaking Scots) is taught in schools in the area, and many children still learn it from their parents. But as Donald Maciver, Gaelic-speaking editor of the Western Isles' weekly newspaper, admitted in 1987, the steady decline in the number of speakers has not been halted: "The reality of it is that the kids in the village who once spoke Gaelic don't nowadays. English is the language of the playground."

Gaelic survives as a literary language, thanks to poets like Sorley McLean, Derick Thomson and Iain Crichton Smith. But efforts to bring it into the world of commerce, politics and technology are painfully difficult. Mr. Maciver's paper, the *Stornoway Gazette*, is published almost entirely in English. The council conducts its debates in English because there are always a few members who can't manage Gaelic. What steps the council has taken—changing all the name signs for towns and villages to Gaelic spelling, for example—often seem to run into obstacles. "Barvas" may be "Barabhas" on the new sign, but it's still Barvas on every available map.

Envious eyes are cast southward to the United Kingdom's other Celtic state-within-a-state, Wales. The Welsh, with hundreds of thousands of native speakers, have their own TV channel. Some Highlanders and Islanders believe more Gaelic TV, beyond the few programs now broadcast, would be just the tonic needed to give the language credibility among the young.

All Scots are familiar with scraps of Gaelic. Some words and phrases have passed into Scottish English, like *slainte-mhath,* a drinking toast, and *ceilidh,* a Highland-style evening of music, dance and drink. Besides, virtually every hill, mountain, river and loch north of the Central Belt has a Gaelic name. Translating these wild-sounding, hard-to-pronounce names into English can make the ancient Gaels less remote to us: They did no more to make themselves feel at home than the early American settlers who christened Little Rock and Salt Lake City. Beinn Dearg, for instance, means Red Mountain; Drumochter, where the main road between Perth and Inverness crosses a high pass, should really be Druimuachdair, meaning Summit Ridge; Loch an Eilean is Island Loch.

But as far as global English is concerned, Gaelic has contributed just one common word by which it can be remembered, particularly in the advertising agencies and campaign offices of the world: "slogan," originally *sluagh ghairm*, the war cry of the Highland clans.

The Scots: Stereotype and Reality

Under the Map

In 1975, the British Government divided Scotland into nine administrative regions. These were named Borders, Dumfries and Galloway, Strathclyde, Central, Lothian, Fife, Tayside, Grampian and Highland. The Western Isles, Orkney and Shetland were given their own local councils.

But how far do these lines on the map, based on layers of older lines stretching back beyond the Picts, reflect the Scots' own sense of identity? From Stranraer in the far southwest to Thurso on the north coast, people will cheer on the same Scottish national soccer team. And yet, as in any country, they have more local loyalties. There are loyalties to family, to village, to town, to area; loyalties to religion; loyalties to working community, be it distilling, trawling or shipbuilding. And there are certainly some in Scotland who prefer not to think of themselves as Scots at all. Risky as it is to characterize any place in terms of majority traits, it is worth trying to peel away the neat print of the paper map and look at the complex patterns of real human beings beneath.

First some cautious words on the Scots in general. By world standards—even by the standards of Europe, Japan and North America—they are a well-educated people. The "school-for-all" system dates back centuries, and two of Scotland's eight universities (Glasgow and St. Andrews) were founded before Columbus's fateful voyage across the Atlantic. Although their position, tucked away in a distant corner of Europe, might once have kept the Scots out of touch with the world, since the eighteenth century they have had a global outlook. Generations of emigration mean few Scots are without relatives in faraway countries such as New Zealand or Canada. The world's output of books, TV and film reaches them as quickly as anyone else nowadays, and the era of affordable air travel has put destinations like Spain and Greece on ordinary Scots' vacation maps. On average, Scots read more newspapers than any other European people.

The Scots' view of themselves tends to be a mixture of outrageous pride and cynical put-downs of their ability to get things right. Mixture means just that: The complete Scottish patriot is a far rarer animal than in England or the United States, and tends to be viewed as something of a clown, while any Scot who writes off his or her native land completely will be disliked. Characteristic Scots can never praise Scotland without a hint of irony in their voice, and can never criticize it without betraying their love for the place.

Certain features might seem to mark the Scots as an unemotional people, unwilling to expose in public any excitement or passion they might feel: a restraint even among close friends will not, as a rule, allow them to kiss or hold hands or generally touch each other in public, as other peoples often do; a tendency toward a cynical, deadpan style of humor; a reluctance to express enthusiasm for anything in direct terms—thus, "It's no bad" becomes the equivalent of "It's wonderful!" But to describe this as unemotional behavior would be simplistic. All public displays of emotion are relative. It may be that outside observers simply have to tune their antennas to more subtle signals.

There are, however, historical reasons why modern Scots might remain shy of being quickly and obviously moved to passion. One is that, since Scottish history began, Scotland's people have been promised much and given little. Through centuries of ceaseless war and famine, to present-day oil slump and unemployment, the Scots have grown wary and skeptical toward any apparently bright prospect held out to them. The other reason relates to religion. When in 1560 the laid-back, free-and-easy moral climate of the old Scottish Catholic Church was replaced by the strict teachings of Calvinist Protestantism, it was as if a red-hot iron had been plunged into a tub of icy water. For the Calvinists, there was no straightforward confession of sins: If a person repented on the deathbed, it was too late. You either lived a good life or you roasted in hell for eternity. This teaching did not cure the Scots of sin, but left them with an abiding feeling, which lasts to this day, that punishment automatically goes hand in hand with most kinds of enjoyment. The everyday implications of this vague feeling were summed up for the author when he overheard an Edinburgh mother tell her complaining son, as she vigorously toweled him down after a swim, "You've had the pleasure long enough to suffer."

On many occasions, of course—at New Year, at weddings, at parties, at major soccer games—Scots will dance, sing, kiss, embrace, cheer and generally let themselves go as much as anyone. They also have a tendency to sentimentality. When any number are gathered together, looking back on a history of lost causes and what-might-have-beens can bring on a communal feeling of general lament. Add music, and the combination is unerring in its effect. While the bulk of Scotland's

Almost 250 years after the Clearances, the hereditary clan chiefs are mostly educated in English or Anglo-Scottish private schools, and clan gatherings have become synthetic spectacles such as this one in Edinburgh's Princes Street Gardens. Scotsman Publications Ltd.

population would not describe themselves as folk-music fans, such songs have a power to bring a lump to any Scot's throat. To sit in a Scottish pub at the end of the evening when a singer strikes up the opening of the song "Flower of Scotland," to see the moist eyes of grown men as they join in, is to realize the true depth of the Scots' feelings for their homeland.

The outside world has two contrasting sets of clichés to apply to the

Scots. One portrays them as a quaint, rural people, honest and friendly, dressed in tartan and kilt, fond of the sound of the bagpipes, simple yet shrewd, clever with their hands and cautious with their money, living slow, antiquated lives in a wet country covered with heather and ruined castles. The other view—confined more to the English—casts them as tough, violent city dwellers with incomprehensible accents, living for the most part in poverty, mean with their money and far too fond of their drink. Both images are misconceptions but contain grains of truth. While the Scots dislike being stereotyped as much as anyone else, they feel it is important for the outside world to have some idea of what makes Scotland special, however distorted. And it is a matter of pride for the Scots to cherish and act on some of these traditions.

The kilt is a good example. Historically a sheet of cloth worn in a fashion resembling the clothing of the ancient Greeks or Romans, its use was confined to the Highlands. The modern kilt is closer to a pleated tartan skirt and has seldom been worn as an everyday item of clothing except by Scottish soldiers serving in the British army. Yet the Scots keep a place for it in certain special areas of life, wearing it without embarrassment and without any intention of impressing tourists. Clothes normally follow the standard European pattern; a visitor could sit on a bench in the middle of Edinburgh for a whole afternoon and not see one man in a kilt. Any tartan spotted is just as likely to be on a scarf around the neck of an American visitor. But even Scots who have never worn them before will proudly display rented kilts at weddings or black-tie dinner parties. Most Scottish regiments in the British army wear kilts on ceremonial occasions, and in events at Highland Games such as "tossing the caber"—throwing a log so it lies in a certain way—competitors will wear kilts.

What of the more negative images of Scotland? There is no truth in the idea that Scots are miserly. If they have a reputation for tightfistedness, it stems from two historical conditions. One is that Scotland was, and is, poorer on average than most other European nations. The other is similar to that which unjustly gave the Jews their reputation for penny-pinching. In the eighteenth and nineteenth centuries many Scots became successful businessmen and entrepreneurs, at home and overseas. Envious people outside Scotland slurred their success by branding them misers—when in fact they simply knew how to work capitalism better.

Where violence and alcohol are concerned, the truth is much the same. As a race the Scots are not cursed with some genetic trait that leads them to drink and fight more than other people. It is nothing unique to Scotland that men and women seek an escape from poverty and monotony through drink. Certainly, as elsewhere, there is a high degree of public, commercial and government hypocrisy reflected in society's universal condemnation of illegal narcotic drugs while one of the most dangerous depressant drugs, alcohol, is legally promoted and consumed. At the same time, for all classes, drinking is a sociable activity. Scotland has many public houses, or pubs, serving alcoholic drink to anyone aged eighteen and over. Undoubtedly some, particularly those catering to the affluent young, do foster violence. But others, at their best, provide a friendly focus for community life through such activities as charitable fund-raising and organizing amateur sports teams. In the late 1980's there has been increasing concern in both Scotland and England about the high number of drink-related crimes; the response has been an encouragingly effective clamp-down on drunk driving and a widening public acceptance of such products as low-alcohol beer.

The worst that can be said to support the image of the brawling, drunken Scot is that some Scotsmen like to maintain the idea that they are tougher and can hold their drink better than foreigners, especially the English. Men will be encouraged and expected to drink more than

Evening in a typical Scottish pub.   Scotsman Publications

is good for them as a mark of virility, and in some groups respect for the "hard men" goes too far toward respect for violence. But again, Scotland is scarcely unique in this.

Scotsmen and Scotswomen

Women's position in Scottish society, and the role of the family, has very much followed the pattern of the Western world in general since the First World War. In Scotland, however, the idea of the woman as wage earner predated the munitions factories of 1914–1918 by more than a century. The textile factories of the west, the jute mills of Dundee, the herring-processing industry—all these provided women with a small degree of economic independence. While it did not free them from the assumed necessity of marriage, childbearing and housework, it helped give the Scottish mother a position of authority in the family, which she retains today. A popular Scottish cartoon strip about an ordinary Dundee family, the Broons (the Browns), shows the relative sizes of "Maw" Broon and "Paw" Broon to be about three to one. Though the strip is to an extent stuck in a 1950's time warp, it demonstrates a truth about who wears the trousers in many Scots households.

Scots can marry young: The law allows anyone aged sixteen to marry, although not to vote or to drink until the age of eighteen. Many Scots do in fact marry as teenagers, although the early twenties is a more usual age. At the same time a relatively liberal moral climate (liberal compared with the repressive atmosphere of the 1950's and before) allows more acceptance of people living together outside marriage.

Women won the vote soon after the First World War, and have gradually forced open the door to equality. Although employers are now forbidden by law to bar women from all but a few jobs, male chauvinism persists at all levels of society; skilled trades like mining and steelmaking have no women employees, and women are lower paid on average than men. But in certain areas—professions such as medicine, law, journalism, accountancy—women are rising through the ranks. And the ratio of women to men at some universities and colleges is approaching or exceeding the fifty–fifty mark.

Living Together, Living Apart

Rural Scotland

According to the population figures, Scotland is much less crowded than most West European countries. It has an average of 172 people for every square mile of land (66 per sq. km.); the English are crammed together more than five times as densely.

But the figures are misleading. Scotland's population is not spread evenly. Four out of five Scots live in the Central Belt, which occupies scarcely a third of the country's area; and half of these are concentrated in Strathclyde, the region that contains Glasgow and its numerous satellite communities. In short, most people in Scotland live in cities and towns.

The poverty of much of Scotland's soil is another pointer toward the lifestyle of its people. Half the country's land is barren, boggy or suitable only for rough grazing. A mere 2 percent of working people are involved in agriculture, forestry and fishing, compared with 25 percent in manufacturing and 60 percent in service industries (although the manufacturing figure includes such major rural industries as whisky production—most distilleries are based in the countryside or in small towns).

For those who do work the land and sea for a living, produce varies widely from region to region. In the southwest and center of the country, dairy farms are common. On the east coast, where the land is more fertile, is a patchwork of farmland fit for plowing. There is not enough sunshine for bread-flour-quality wheat to thrive, but lower-grade wheat is grown. Other cereal crops are oats and barley (important to the brewing and distilling industry). The main root crops are rutabagas (known as turnips or *neeps* in Scotland) and potatoes (*tatties*). Mainstays of farming communities on the rolling slopes north and west of Dundee are raspberries and strawberries; scientists working on the outskirts of the city have produced a hybrid fruit, the "Tayberry."

The potato and berry harvests can affect the timing of school vacations. Farmers depend on schoolchildren, itinerant workers and poor families to gather the crops. The berries usually ripen during the long summer school vacation, but in Tayside, schools take an extra fortnight's break during the autumn semester so the potatoes can be gathered—the process of *tattie howkin'*.

The northeast is renowned for its beef: The Aberdeen Angus breed is famous worldwide. But the animal that dominates the Scottish farming scene is the sheep. The introduction of these animals in great numbers to Scotland two hundred years ago is inextricably linked to the cruel forced exodus that emptied the Highlands of people (These "clearances" are discussed more fully in Chapter XIII.) But the country has come to terms with these docile, hardy beasts since then. More important than their meat is their wool, which is used by Scotland's knitwear industry and the tweed makers of the Western Isles. The value of sheep

Copper whisky-pot stills of traditional shape at the Glenfiddich distillery, near Dufftown, Grampian. Andrew Stevens

Drink

Scotland's national drink, of course, is Scotch whisky (only non-Scotch should be spelled "whiskey"). The name comes from the Gaelic words *uisge beatha*, meaning "water of life," and the spirit began as the product of domestic Highland stills. From the eighteenth century on, government customs officers fought a running battle with illegal whisky makers trying to avoid high taxes on alcohol. But by the Victorian era, legal manufacturers were starting large-scale production. Today there are more than a hundred Scottish distilleries, from Orkney to Wigtown, producing distinctively flavored malt whiskies: well-known brands like Glenfiddich, Glenlivet and Glenmorangie, and less familiar ones like Bunnahabhain and Springbank. Pure "single malts" are mixed together with Lowland grain whiskies to make the other type of Scotch, the "blended whisky."

Here is how one malt is made, at the Glenfiddich Distillery near Dufftown: Malted barley, ground to a powder, is mixed with springwater and heated in a "mash tun." A sugary liquid called "wort" results. Yeast is added and the liquid fermented in massive wooden tubs called "washbacks" until it resembles beer. This is bled off to copper stills and distilled twice. The final fluid is then stored in oak casks, maturing for a minimum of eight years before being diluted with more springwater and bottled for sale.

to the landowner is that they can be left to graze on the steep, infertile, rock-strewn hills that make up so much of the countryside and would otherwise be unproductive.

In addition to such conventional farmers, there exists a different kind of worker of the land: the crofter. "Croft" refers both to the crofter's dwelling and to the small farm that is worked. Crofting communities are confined to the Highlands and islands. Each crofter has an individual patch of land for growing vegetables or cereals, and another, much larger area of land is used for communal grazing. In areas where peat is burned for fuel, each village's "grazing committee" also allocates where each crofter can cut peat.

These days crofting tends to be a spare-time activity, with few people relying on their crofts for food. At most, crofts provide their tenants with extra income to supplement a main wage, or to tide them over between seasonal jobs. Nevertheless, a crofting village remains an intriguing sight: low, sturdy houses of stone or plastered brick, with farmland running right up to front doors uninterrupted by gardens or hedges, and brown slices of peat piled neatly in head-high stacks against one wall.

While some look to the land, others look outward to the sea. Scotland has more than eight thousand working fishermen, with twice that number employed in the fish-processing industry onshore. This is a fraction of the figure at the beginning of the twentieth century, when the export of herring—the "silver darlings"—to eastern Europe was at its peak.

Fishing still plays a lead role in many coastal towns, however. Aberdeen and Peterburgh in the northeast are the most important fishing ports, followed by Fraserburgh, Macduff and Buckie (on the Moray Firth); Lerwick, capital of Shetland; and the west's Ullapool, Kinlochbervie, Mallaig and Ayr. Apart from herring, the main catches are mackerel, haddock, cod, whiting, crab and lobster.

Most Scottish fishermen work on a profit-share basis. What cash remains after running expenses are accounted for is divided between members of a boat's crew and those owning a share in that particular vessel.

Crofter on Lemreway, Isle of Lewis. Eolas/Sam Maynard

tants a reputation for hard, squalid living that is proving difficult to shake off.

There is always a dilemma in writing about Glasgow. To stress the city's grimmer side is to underplay its attractions. Glasgow has a rich, cosmopolitan cultural life—it has generated Scotland's best recent novelists, it hosts the Scottish Opera Company and one of the world's most innovative theaters. Many of its inhabitants remain prosperous, and determined efforts are being made to improve the worst housing.

On the other hand, it is too easy to be dazzled by the glitzy "theme" pubs of the West End, the stylish clothes and hairstyles of Glasgow's trendsetters and the busy modern uptown shopping malls, and forget the many underprivileged people on the city outskirts.

With Edinburgh, Scotland's capital and its second largest city, the

Nineteenth-century tenements in Leith, Edinburgh. The cobbles seen here paving Pitt Street are retained more for sentimental than practical reasons, as elsewhere in the Scottish capital. Author

The center of Edinburgh today, with Princes Street on the right and Edinburgh Castle at the top left. The spiky building in the foreground is the Scott Monument. Scottish Tourist Board

situation is reversed. While Glasgow labors under an unqualified reputation for urban decay, Edinburgh enjoys its image as one of Europe's most beautiful cities. So it is—but it, too, has its seamier aspect.

Edinburgh, home to more than 400,000 people (compared with Glasgow's 700,000 plus), is built on the land between the Pentland Hills and the southern shores of the Firth of Forth. Its nucleus is Castle Rock, a craggy, soot-blackened massif topped by the thick walls and battlements of Edinburgh Castle. Sloping down east of the castle is the Old Town, the original heart of Edinburgh. At the foot of the rock to the north, on the site of a drained loch, is the so-called New Town (actually built over two hundred years ago).

Edinburgh is one of Europe's leading financial centers. It also boasts the headquarters of two of the three Scottish banks, and is the home of Scotland's highest court, the Court of Session. But it is not purely the pretty, legal-financial-academic, white-collar tourist haven many visitors and not a few of its inhabitants imagine. Although it has never had the tradition of heavy industry attached to the west coast, Edinburgh has many factories and its own major port. Most of Scotland's remaining coal mines lie close to the city. And there are many problems associated with poverty, unemployment and bad housing to be tackled—Edinburgh has Scotland's worst AIDS problem, for example, thanks primarily to drug takers sharing syringes—before all the city's inhabitants participate in the prosperity of the center and the wealthy suburbs.

Aberdeen is less than half as big as Edinburgh, and lies well to the north of the Central Belt. Facing the open sea, it is surrounded on three sides by the rich farmland of the Grampian region. It is sometimes known as the Granite City: Many buildings are made out of the local gray granite. The durability of this toughest of building materials is astonishing. Resistant to pollution and to the general erosion of the elements, buildings put up in Victorian times look as though they were completed yesterday.

Once the capital of a region devoted to the production of food and whisky, Aberdeen—and the lives of its inhabitants—has been transformed by the discovery of massive reserves of oil under the North Sea. Aberdeen is now the oil capital of Britain. Many a Texan boot crosses the concourse of Aberdeen airport, and the rail station sees work-hungry oilmen from all over Britain going to and from their long, hard spells on the offshore production rigs. Supply ships compete with fishing vessels for space in the harbor, and the need to ferry crews quickly between shore and rig has made Aberdeen the world's busiest heliport. The discovery of oil has also made property more and more expensive for local people trying to buy their first homes—and Aberdonians are aware that the wealth the boom has brought will last only as long as the oil keeps flowing.

Dundee, a little smaller than Aberdeen, is situated on the steeply sloping north bank of the Firth of Tay. It is sometimes said that the way the city is built makes the worst possible use of the best possible location. It is true that even today architects and property developers are not prevented from dumping ugly buildings where they spoil the look of the city. But Dundee can still be a fine sight, particularly when approached from either of the two bridges spanning the Tay, and particularly at night, when its long, thin shape stretches across the horizon, picked out in orange streetlights, making it seem a far bigger metropolis than it really is. The bridges have become two of Dundee's best-known trademarks. The road bridge, built in the 1960's, is among the world's longest. The railway bridge was built in the Victorian era as a replacement for the infamous original, which collapsed during a storm in 1879 as a train crammed with passengers was crossing it.

Dundee lies roughly at equal distances from Glasgow, Edinburgh and Aberdeen. But this has not made it any kind of crossroads, and Dundonians often feel frustration at living in Scotland's forgotten city. Too far north to feed off the economic heartland of the Central Belt, too far south to benefit more than marginally from North Sea oil, too far east to be the tourist gateway to the Highlands (a position enjoyed by Perth and Glasgow), Dundee faces a continual struggle to find a role. Once known as a major whaling port, a center for foreign trade and the city of the "three J's"—jute, jam and journalism—Dundee has been hit by successive slumps in the world economy. An effort is now under way between the city's council and various government agencies to encourage new industries to settle in specially created business zones. But just as important as jobs in persuading Dundonians not to leave their native city is fostering a sense of pride and identity with the place. Moreover, what nightlife and entertainment the city has to offer is only now catching up with the caliber of education available—namely, a university, an art school turning out some of Scotland's best artists and one of Europe's finest teaching hospitals.

The New Towns

Alongside Scotland's traditional communities, five "new towns" have been set up since the end of the Second World War. All are in the Central Belt. Meant to ease the overcrowding of Glasgow, they were also intended to give businesses room to expand where and how they liked, free from the maze of planning regulations and clogged-up, narrow streets that bedevil European firms based in cities built before the invention of the automobile. These new towns, with their young populations, neat modern housing and carefully landscaped industrial estates, are only now coming of age. It is too soon to say whether a new kind of Scot is emerging from this environment.

Livingston, 15 miles (24 km.) west of Edinburgh, is a new town founded in 1962. It has a population of more than 40,000. For some, the town has provided a fresh start, a good job, a first home, a chance to bring up a family in clean, green surroundings far removed from the fume-choked stone jungle of the traditional cities. Livingston's representative in the British parliament, Robin Cook, tells a story about a TV crew that came to film at a community recreation center in the town and was so astonished at the lack of graffiti, it had some specially sprayed onto a plasterboard prop.

At the same time, Livingston's inhabitants have problems adapting to the new lifestyle. Unemployment is surprisingly high, newcomers can find it a struggle to cope without relatives close at hand and places to gather and socialize are scarce. The Livingstonians' typically Scottish liking for public transport also clashes with the ideals of town planners.

The town was designed for car owners, but a third of households do not have cars.

Forces for Disunity: Regional

From the network of Scottish living and working environments thus sketched, it is possible to draw a hazy and very approximate version of the Scots' own mental map of their country. Putting imaginary names to these shorthand concepts, Scotland could be split into six parts: North Britain, the Industrial Republic, Pictland, Aberdeen, the Highlands and the Arctic Fringe.

North Britain
This area would cover the Lothian region, including Edinburgh, plus the Borders, Central, and most of the Dumfries and Galloway regions. It is seen by Scots as the most English-oriented part of the country, the most integrated into the United Kingdom as a whole, the most prosperous and politically right wing. Its own middle and upper classes see it as the national center of culture, learning, finance and national administration. The last two are borne out by the facts, to some extent; the first two are not. And "North Britain" has areas of major industry in its own right.

The Industrial Republic
This is essentially Strathclyde south of Helensburgh, plus parts of the Central region. This name conveys the distinct self-consciousness felt by its people, a clear sense that they are West Coasters as well as Scots, born of a proud industrial heritage, guardians of a unique working-class culture. In the rest of Scotland the area has a somewhat grimy, tough image—an image that many of the inhabitants of Glasgow, Paisley, Clydebank and Motherwell are in no hurry to dispel. There is an undisputed rivalry between this area and "North Britain," particularly between Glasgow and Edin-

The ever-changing kaleidoscope of clouds, rain and sunshine above the mountains of the northwest Highlands. Author

burgh, although this is as likely to show itself in contests to see who can win the title of Scotland's cultural capital as in blue-collar/white-collar hostility.

Pictland

Actually no one in Scotland feels any great affinity with the country's oldest inhabitants, but ancient Pictland covered an area that tends to be perceived today as a whole by many Scots: the northeast, including Fife, Tayside and rural Grampian. It is seen as a fertile land with a gentle climate, a land of farmers, distillerymen and fishermen, a land where events happen at a slow pace and on a small scale. In reality, of course, Dundee and the mining and manufacturing towns of southern Fife are there, too. Dundee's identity crisis has already been mentioned; the proximity of Fife to the Central Belt means its people are inclined to focus on Glasgow and Edinburgh as the pivot on which their Scotland turns. Perhaps Grampian is the part of this imaginary Pictland with the strongest independent identity, with its pattern of closely linked small towns, villages and farms and the distinctive dialect of its people.

Aberdeen

As already described, Aberdeen is a city transformed by North Sea oil, and is still perceived by Scotland—oil-price slump or not—as something of an international boom town.

Highlands

The affection of the Scots for this bleak and beautiful wilderness has been mentioned in the previous chapter. Scots tend to think of it as devoid of people save crofters and hoteliers, and it is true that less than 300,000 people live there. But not all of them have crofts or cater to the tourist trade: Employers range from the Forestry Commission to the United Kingdom Atomic Energy Authority. There is also a high level of unemployment. The Highlanders' reluctance to jeopardize job opportunities can lead to clashes with environmentalists, seen as interfering southern do-gooders. A recent example involved an English TV naturalist, who was forced to back down from his campaign to preserve an Islay peat bog used by wild geese when local people supported a plan to cut the peat for the furnaces of a whisky distillery. Episodes like this, and a degree of resentment over their country being used as a summer playground (much of the Highlands belongs to absentee landowners), means the historic differences between the Highlanders and other Scots linger on. To the Lewis crofter or the Ullapool fish farmer, there is really not much difference between being governed by London and governed by Edinburgh.

The Arctic Fringe

The same attitude prevails in Orkney and Shetland, which became part of the Kingdom of Scotland a scant 131 years before it was joined to the Kingdom of England. They do not speak Gaelic in these northern archipelagoes, and have as much in common with Scandinavia as they do with the Western Isles. But, like the Highlanders, they wonder whether an independent Scotland would rule them any more fairly than the British government does. This feeling is particularly strong in Shetland, where a political party, the Shetland Movement, has already won seats on the islands' council. From the point of view of southern Scots, Orkney and Shetland seem remote because they *are*, even as holiday destinations. To put this in perspective, a 1987 travel brochure quoted a price of over $600 for a seven-day vacation in Shetland, flying from Glasgow or Edinburgh. For the same price a Scot could have at least a fortnight in southern Spain or Greece.

Forces for Disunity

Religion

The dominant Scottish branch of Christianity is Protestant, represented most often by the wholly independent Church of Scotland, the "Kirk." On the west coast there are a number of more fundamentalist Protestant groups, whose members live much more strictly according to their interpretation of the word of God. These churches hark back to the dawn of Protestantism in the sixteenth century, when Scotland was swept by religious fervor. Even today the Isle of Lewis virtually shuts down on Sundays, with many of its inhabitants frowning on any kind of Sabbath work or play.

Scotland also has a large Catholic minority, also centered on the west coast, although Catholic communities can be found in all Scottish towns and cities. Many Irish Catholics emigrated to Scotland—just a few miles away from Ireland by ferry—in the nineteenth century. Catholic and Protestant children attend separate schools, although both are administered by the same local authorities. In some areas—notably in Coatbridge, an industrial town of some 50,000 people just east of Glasgow, Catholicism is the dominant religion.

Normally Protestants and Catholics live and work contentedly together. But, as it does so often in Western Europe, the burden of history sometimes manages to pull different communities apart. A Glaswegian Protestant and a Glaswegian Catholic who marry can still find themselves shunned by their families. This sad situation is kept alive by folk memory, by the division of education, and by two more complicated factors.

The first is the continuing strife in Ireland. In the six counties of Northern Ireland, still a part of the United Kingdom, a Protestant majority confronts a Catholic minority aggrieved by past discrimination and oppression. Links between the Northern Ireland Catholics and Protestants and their sister communities in Scotland remain strong. The death and destruction wrought as terrorists, sympathizers and British soldiers clash in Northern Ireland makes young Scots all the more conscious of what church they "belong to," and perpetuates the division between the communities.

Sports

The other factor, and the arena in which this division occasionally opens into violence, is soccer—the Scottish national sport. Three of the big cities have two major soccer teams each. Historically, one is the Catholic team, the other the Protestant. The biggest pair, predictably, is based in Glasgow: Celtic and Rangers. Their rivalry is so established that they share a single nickname, the "Old Firm." For a Protestant to support Celtic or a Catholic to support Rangers is virtually unthinkable. To its credit, Celtic has had Protestants on its team. In the summer of 1989, Rangers astonished Scotland by ending its tradition of not signing Catholic players. It paid almost $2.5 million for the outstanding Catholic center-forward Maurice "Mo" Johnston, who had a few weeks earlier been about to sign for Celtic. Perhaps the rift is slowly beginning to close, but in the meantime the fans hurl their religion at each other as taunts and rallying cries.

Forces for Change

Some of the ways Scottish society is altering have already been hinted at, and others will be discussed in later chapters. But worth mentioning here are two key forces for change that are directly affecting Scots today and will continue doing so for years to come.

One force is deindustrialization, the painful process that has seen the pride of Scottish manufacturing industry—shipbuilding, heavy engineering, steelmaking—shrink and fade in the face of foreign competition. This has hurt the Scots, who know their country rose to world renown in the nineteenth century on the back of their reputation for engineering. The growth of the electronics industry along the Glasgow-Edinburgh corridor—forming a so-called "Silicon Glen"—and the massive increase in service industries such as finance, retail and tourism have not yet healed this wound.

Some say the Scots have a sentimental, overromanticized view of their industrial past. All right, they argue, the shipyards are almost all shut, the steel industry is on the brink, coal mining has contracted. But this is all part of natural evolution, and Scots must learn to adapt to the industries of the future.

It is true that the Scots cannot live by producing ships or machinery the world does not want. But if modern Scots do look back regretfully

Work finishes on an oil rig at the once-mighty Scott Lithgow yard in Greenock, on the Clyde. Already on its knees following the collapse of the shipbuilding industry, the oil slump of the 1980's hit Scott Lithgow hard. A few days after this picture was taken, in 1987, hundreds of men were laid off, and the yard was mothballed indefinitely. Author

to the years when their country was in the vanguard of Victorian industry, it is with some justification. For another difference between then and now is that products like the liners and freighters and battle-ships that left the Clyde were not only built by Scots, but designed by them. More and more Scots find that their employers in the new indus-tries, which are to some extent replacing the old, have head offices not in Edinburgh or even London but in Japan and the United States. IBM, for example, built a new plant at Greenock as the Scott Lithgow ship-yard there entered its death throes. The plant has its own designers and scientists, many of them Scottish, and Scotland can feel proud that it was selected as the site for a key high-technology base. But the fact remains that all major decisions affecting its future are made across the Atlantic by non-Scots. Scots are increasingly having to come to terms with a loss of economic, as well as political, independence.

The other force for change is Scotland's declining population. Emigration has always been a fact of Scottish life. In one decade alone—the 1960's—Scotland lost 6 percent of its people through emigration to England and the rest of the world. Then, the loss was made up through a relatively high birth rate. But now, with Scots still taking the traditional path to opportunity overseas, the birth rate has slowed. The country's population is set to fall well below the five million mark by the year 2000. Optimists suggest this is bound to make Scotland a better place to live: more space, less unemployment, less pressure on housing. Pessimists point out that many of those leaving the country are its best and brightest. Nationalists fear that prospects for independence dwindle with every thousand-person fall in population.

Forces for Unity

A common language, a common soccer team; their own legal system, their own educational system, their own banknotes. Are these enough to bind the Scots together, to let them call themselves a nation? The voice of the emigrant Scot can be heard, holding forth to an audience, perhaps some friends in a Toronto social club, or nephews at a Melbourne barbecue. The voice tells of a Scotland that has beautiful scenery; whose people are honest, friendly and hard-working, if a little gloomy at times, who treat each other as equals in a way their English neighbors do not. The emigrant's description reveals a view of himself and of his native land shared by many Scots abroad; but it is simplified, perhaps a little rose-tinted, by distance. In the day-to-day realities of modern Scottish life, a richer and more complex pattern of shared experience can be traced, as the next chapter shows.

A Day in the Life of Scotland

A lot can happen in a country in twenty-four hours. So many departures and arrivals, births and deaths, triumphs and disasters. But just so long as the focus is not on individuals, one of the best ways to look at the routines, patterns and institutions of ordinary life in Scotland is to follow the country through a single, typical working day. Say it is Wednesday, October 31: The day is about to begin.

Four A.M.: Home

Most of Scotland is asleep. Not all, though. Farmers and crofters, fishermen too perhaps, are beginning the first chores of the day. In the sorting offices of the Royal Mail—Britain's postal service—letters and parcels are prepared for delivery. In a control room at Prestwick, near Ayr, air-traffic controllers monitor the steady stream of airliners flying between Canada and Scotland on the busiest air route between North America and Europe. Doctors and nurses patrol the darkened hospital wards of the National Health Service, the British organization that provides all Scots with free health care, funded by income tax.

But most of Scotland is asleep at home. Home can mean many things—a tiny single-story cottage in a Fife fishing village; a country mansion; an apartment in a nineteenth-century city tenement block, six flights up.

A typical Scottish family house will be made of stone if it was built before the First World War, brick if it is more recent. It will have a small garden, and may be part of a row of similarly designed houses called a "terrace." Some stone houses and almost all brick ones are given a coating of cement, which is painted or studded with tiny stones. The roof will usually be covered with slate. A characteristic feature of the Scottish house is the double door—a stout outer door, a small porch, and a lighter inner door—to keep out cold winters.

Home for more than half Scotland's households is a "council house," a dwelling built and leased by a local civic authority, usually one of the democratically elected "district councils." Rents are subsidized. Council houses first began to be built in the 1920's. They vary widely. Most were designed with high ideals of providing people with a good place to live. The best resemble the ideal family home described above, and much council housing in the new towns falls into this category.

But all too often carefully planned "estates" of council houses were badly built. Design details that would have made them more pleasant to live in, such as public parks and gardens or ornamental doors and windows, were left out to save money. Shops, pubs and recreation facilities were not provided along with the houses. Architects would forget the need for individuals to feel their homes were different, separate, unique; and a drab monotony settled over estates where every dwelling was the same. The worst examples came in the 1960's and 1970's, when town planners saw the ideal solution to the housing shortage in building tower blocks of steel and concrete—a style of architecture virtually unknown in Scotland up to that point. These "multistoreys," or "multis," as they came to be called, sprang up on the outskirts of major cities and towns. Most were poorly designed, and not enough money was invested in their construction. Few took account of the damp Scottish climate. Residents were not provided with adequate security from crime. The multis have become a byword in Scotland for uncomfortable living conditions. Rather than invest in making them pleasant places to live—as many could be, with proper weatherproofing, economical heating, noise insulation between apartments, well-lit interiors and a large caretaking staff—councils prefer to replace them with modern versions of traditional ground-level homes.

Seven Thirty A.M.: Off to Work

Many Scottish hotels send guests on their way in the morning with what they call a "traditional Scots breakfast," a gigantic meal of toast and marmalade, bacon and eggs, kippers and tea. How traditional this has ever been for the bulk of Scotland's population is doubtful. But two traditions do remain: tea and porridge. Despite the advance of instant coffee, tea remains the drink that starts most Scots off in the mornings and keeps them going through the day. It is usually made in a pot with leaf tea or large teabags (not the fiddly little bags with strings attached that are common in America) and drunk from mugs with milk and sugar. Porridge, a heated mixture of water and oatmeal, survives as a popular breakfast dish. Traditionally it is eaten with salt rather than sugar. Just as tea battles to hold its own against coffee, so porridge has become less popular with the advent of cold breakfast cereals.

Getting to work involves the mix of transport common to most modern societies—bus, train and car. Only Glasgow has a subway, a small loop serving the center of the city. (Because of the way Scottish cities have developed over hundreds of years, with new rings being added to a central, ancient core, Scots tend to talk about the "town center" rather than "downtown.")

Many Scottish households own one or more cars. New roads are constantly being built and improved, with the result that the country is now well served with a network of freeways ("motorways" and "dual carriageways") and ordinary two-lane roads. On the fastest roads cars are allowed to travel at 70 miles (110 km.) per hour. As in the rest of Britain, motorists drive on the left. Scarcely any cars or trucks are made in Scotland: Scots drive vehicles made in England, continental Europe and Japan. Scottish towns were founded long before the automobile was invented, and their centers contain numerous alleyways and tight corners through which big cars find it difficult to maneuver; thus cars tend to be smaller than in America.

Many Scots travel to work or school on buses. In towns and cities these are often double-decker buses, built, as their name implies, with an extra passenger deck on top of the normal one.

The railways in Scotland are run by a single government-owned organization called British Rail. Its mixture of diesel and electric trains covers far less territory than in the heyday of the railways (some quite important towns, such as St. Andrews, no longer have rail links), but major urban centers are all served by train. The busiest stations, Edinburgh Waverley and Glasgow Central, have all the bustle of small regional airports in the States.

Nine A.M.: School and College

It's heads down in the classrooms and lecture halls as Scotland's students begin the work of the day. Although the country has a haphazard mixture of public, private and volunteer-run kindergartens, education for young Scots starts in earnest at age four or five, with seven years of basic learning at a primary school. Children will be taught reading, writing and arithmetic, and gain early experience in other skills such as the arts, crafts and sciences.

After primary school the eleven- and twelve-year-olds move up to secondary schools. These have between five hundred and a thousand students, drawn from a number of the primaries, which are smaller. Most schools are "comprehensives," meaning that children of either sex and of any ability are admitted.

Children must stay in full-time education until they are sixteen, so the earliest they can leave is at the end of their fourth year at secondary school. The longest they can stay is for six years.

The typical secondary-school day begins with a ten-minute registration period for individual classes at nine P.M. Most students will attend one assembly a week also, where they will gather in the school hall or gymnasium to be addressed by the principal—*rector* in Scotland. Children will then disperse to their various subject classes. Most Scottish schools still make children wear a formal school uniform, consisting of a colored blazer with a school badge, a special school tie, a white shirt or blouse and a gray-flannel skirt or pants.

The school day normally ends at about four P.M., after eight forty-minute subject periods. Scottish schoolchildren get eleven vacation weeks a year—two at Christmas, two at Easter, six in the summer and one other.

During their first two years at secondary school, students (usually

Students at Our Lady's High School, Motherwell, take part in a radio play. Most Scottish schoolchildren still wear uniforms; each school has its own tie and blazer badge. Scotsman Publications Ltd.

referred to as "pupils" until they start at college) study a wide range of subjects. At the end of this period they decide what areas of learning they are most interested in, and spend the next two years working toward their "Standard Grade" qualifications. In each subject, pupils are assessed on a mixture of practical and written work and a final examination. Less able pupils will study for perhaps two or three Standard Grades, the most able for seven or more. A typical mix of subjects would be English, mathematics, history, French, computer studies and art and design. Most schools would be able to offer about twenty further alternatives, including such areas as Gaelic, Russian, drama and economics.

Before Standard Grades were introduced in the late 1980's, whether pupils stood or fell was based entirely on single examinations in each subject at the end of their fourth secondary-school year. Now children who find it hard to prove themselves in written tests have a chance to shine in more practical areas. The English course, for instance, is divided into reading, writing and talking. Math is broken down into knowledge and understanding, reasoning and applications, and investigation.

Compulsory education ends at age sixteen. Some pupils choose to leave school then. They may look for a job straight away, or take combinations of short, practical training courses called "modules" at one of Scotland's fifty or so vocational colleges.

For those who stay on at school, "Higher Grade" subjects are the next step. Pupils will study between three and six of these more advanced courses. Unlike Standard Grades, where pupils can cover a broad range of subjects, picking their "Highers" means they must begin to decide what they are going to specialize in in their future careers.

Pupils can then stay on for one further year, to work toward Certificates of Sixth Year Studies. More challenging and academic, no more than three subjects will be studied as a rule, and an important part of each course is a major assignment involving independent investigation and research into a particular area that interests the pupil.

Armed with good enough Higher or Sixth Year Studies results, or both, pupils can apply for admission to a full-time college or university course. Scotland has eight universities and sixteen full-time colleges offering degree courses of between three and six years' duration.

As in the rest of Britain, but unlike the practice in virtually every other country in the Western world, college and university fees in

Marischal College, Aberdeen University. This Gothic extravaganza in gray granite is a nineteenth-century addition to a university founded more than 500 years ago. Author

Scotland are wholly funded by the government. The government will also pay a fixed sum for students' living expenses, the value of which depends on the wealth of the student's parents.

A typical Scottish university degree course starts with two years in which students can study a wide range of subjects. By this stage they will usually know whether their interests lie toward the arts or sciences, but by no means always: It is not unknown for a student to come to university intending to get a degree in physics, decide he or she doesn't like it, and emerge after four years with a perfectly respectable degree in history.

After examinations at the end of the second year, university students either go on to complete a four-year "Honours" degree course in a single specific subject, or take a three-year "Ordinary" degree without specialization.

Every college and university has its particular strengths and peculiarities. Some specialize right from the start, such as the veterinary or art colleges. Some offer a wide range of courses in restricted areas: Strathclyde and Heriot-Watt universities, for instance, give degrees mainly in the social and physical sciences rather than in the arts. Others have reputations for a particular kind of student body. A high proportion of Glasgow University students, for example, actually live with their families in and around Glasgow; many students at St. Andrews University, by contrast, come from the south of England.

Six P.M.: Food

In most Scottish households, it is time for the main meal of the day—"tea." (In domestic Scotland, lunch is "dinner" and dinner is "tea.")

There are three basic things to say about Scottish food. One is that there are many cherished traditions that go to create a unique national cuisine. The second is that some traditional eating habits of the Scots are dangerously unhealthy. The third is that modern Scotland has available to it an unprecedented choice of international foods, challenging for the first time on a wide scale both the good and bad elements of its traditional diet.

At the heart of all Scottish cooking lies the potato, or "tattie." Boiled, baked, mashed or made into french fries (*chips* to the Scots), it makes a wholesome foundation to any meal. The chip shop, or *chipper*, still provides Scots with their most popular kind of food to go, and one doesn't have to look far in even the smallest town to find one. Their fare does not consist only of fish and chips, but covers many of the meat dishes to be found on the ordinary Scots' tea table—little round thin-crusted mutton pies; sausages; meat-and-potato pasties called *bridies*;

red, white and black puddings (all oatmeal puddings, the last variety made with blood). The rituals remain the same, despite the advent of more exotic foreign items such as Chinese-style spring rolls and smoked sausages. The customer asks for his meal as a "supper"—"Black pudding supper, please." The chips and the pudding, deep fried in batter, are shoveled into a paper bag, salt and vinegar shaken over them, and the bag is wrapped in a page from the previous week's newspaper.

But if there is a dish Scots dream of their mothers making, in the way Americans fondly remember Mom's apple pie, it must be mince and tatties. It could not be simpler: Mince is just the Scottish word for ground beef, usually of as high a quality as in a hamburger. It is fried with onions, simmered in stock and served with boiled or mashed potatoes.

Potatoes form an essential complement to that classic Scottish dish, the haggis. Scottish? Nowadays, perhaps—but the word actually comes from the French *hachis*, meaning finely chopped. John MacSween, Edinburgh's foremost manufacturer and exporter of haggis, describes it as "one of the original convenience foods: a meal in a bag." To make it, butchers take the lungs, heart and liver of a sheep and mince them together with beef fat. This mixture is soaked overnight. Oatmeal, onions, seasoning and gravy are mixed in. The result is put into a tightly sealed bag and boiled for several hours. Traditionally the bag was a sheep's stomach. Nowadays, plastic is often used instead. Haggis must be accompanied by *clapshott*, or "tatties and neeps," a mixture of mashed potato and rutabaga.

Scotland's numerous soup recipes are sadly often confined to restaurants these days, seldom appearing in homemade form on the domestic tea table. The most popular and most likely still to be made at home is Scotch broth, made with mutton stock and whole grains of barley. Other well-known soups include cock-a-leekie, consisting, as its name implies, of chicken and leeks; partan bree, made from crab; and cullen skink, based on smoked haddock.

Scotland's reputation as the "land o'cakes" began on iron griddles over open fires, with oatcakes, bannocks and scones, before moving to the oven. The Scottish baker's repertoire includes shortbread, Dundee cake (a rich, heavy fruit cake) and black bun (a traditional sweet loaf eaten at New Year).

The bakers never run short of customers; nor do the candy stores. Scots are notoriously sweet-toothed. Consumption is high of fizzy drinks (including the legendary, locally produced Irn Bru, which contains small amounts of iron but is not, as its advertisers suggest, "made in Scotland from girders"), cookies, candy bars, and "boiled sweets" (sourballs) sold by the quarter-pound bag from hundreds of different jars in news vendors' stores. The result: Generations of Scots, reared on chocolate, toffee and sugar icing, wave an early farewell to their teeth. Despite a constant campaign to educate young Scots about the danger of too much sugar, the problem continues.

Scotland's other major health problem concerns its general diet. The country has one of the world's highest death rates from heart disease, and this is likely to continue as long as Scots eat so much fatty fried food. People can survive a large number of fried-fish suppers, or break-fasts fried in fat, without keeling over from a heart attack—as long as they balance their diet with healthier food. That message is worryingly slow to penetrate Scotland's consciousness.

Things are changing. For many years a deeply conservative country as far as foreign food was concerned, Scotland has in the past few decades demonstrated an increased willingness to experiment. This willingness has been paralleled by a dramatic widening of choice in terms of raw ingredients available. In the sixties, staple items of European cuisine such as green peppers and garlic were seen as peculiar, alien items. Now every food store offers them, and the major food retail chains compete with each other to stack their shelves with every conceivable variety of international produce. From pumpkins to pumpernickel, from pesto to pakora, Scotland finds itself suddenly overwhelmed with the range of culinary options long taken for granted by such countries as the United States.

Scots have for many years enjoyed certain types of foreign food: Chinese and Italian restaurants are quite common. But the happiest legacy of the vanished British Empire for Scotland has been the numerous Indian restaurants. "Going for a curry" has become a traditional way of ending a night out, whether in a simple restaurant in Stornoway or in the grander surroundings of an upscale establishment in one of the big cities. Glasgow's Indian restaurants, like those of London, are said to rival those of India itself.

Seven P.M.: Leisure, Sport and Celebration

It's time to relax. But not all Scots are going to stay at home watching TV. For some, it is time to stroll down to the local pub. Others are more tense, excited: Tonight is Wednesday night, and that means football. It's also October 31, and that means Halloween. . . .

"Football" is what the Scots call soccer. It has a large following of fervent fans, and a still larger number of occasional supporters. When the Scottish national team plays other countries, particularly England, virtually all Scotland is caught up in the drama.

Football is perhaps the most significant area in which Scotland expresses its independence from the rest of Britain. The sport is administered by the Scottish Football Association (SFA), founded in 1873.

Team football is focused on the Scottish Football League, divided into the Premier, First and Second divisions. During the football season—which lasts from October to May—each team plays all the other teams in its division several times, accumulating points according to whether it wins, loses or draws. At the close of the season, each division will have its champion. The supreme team is the one that accumulates most points in the Premier division, from which it can rise no higher. The best teams in the lower divisions are promoted to the next higher division in the following season; the weakest teams in the higher divisions are relegated to lower ones.

All teams recognized by the SFA, including smaller ones outside the three main divisions, are also eligible for an open knockout competition, the annual Scottish Cup. In practice, end-of-season honors are usually divided among fewer than ten big-city teams, seven of which rarely drop out of the Premier Division—Aberdeen; Dundee United; Dundee; the two Edinburgh teams, Hibernian and Heart of Midlothian ("Hearts"); and of course, the Glasgow "Old Firm" duo of Celtic and Rangers. There is a tremendous gulf between these relatively wealthy clubs, with their big stadiums and dedicated followings of thousands of fans, and the rest of Scottish league football. The $10 million that Rangers spent buying new players during the 1987–88 season would have covered the running costs of most of the teams in the First and Second divisions put together.

The great ambition of every Premier division team has traditionally been to win the "double"—to win the division championship *and* the Scottish Cup in the same year. Now, however, international horizons are widening. There is a third, priceless trophy to win, to make the aim a "treble"—the European Cup. Only the most successful Scottish teams qualify for this, the most important of three annual European competitions. Teams of players from every big European city crisscross the continent in an epic knockout tournament followed eagerly by millions of fans speaking many different languages. The competition knows no political barriers, with Russians, Albanians and Finns all taking part. While Scotland has carried the trophy home just once, when Celtic won it, Scottish teams usually figure strongly in the closing rounds.

The best Scottish players are picked for Scotland's national team, which sets out in its traditional colors of blue and white to do battle around the world, accompanied wherever it goes by a host of fanatical, banner-waving supporters dubbed the "tartan army." Apart from regular contests with England, where the battles of Bannockburn and Culloden are refought in the relatively bloodless arenas of Wembley Stadium in London and Hampden Stadium in Glasgow, the four-year pinnacle of the football calendar is the World Cup.

The World Cup, the greatest of sporting events, followed by billions

Scotland meets England on the soccer field. Here Scottish striker Ally McCoist, on one knee, tries a low cross.   Scotsman Publications Ltd.

of people on TV across the globe, pitches the mighty teams of Europe and Latin America against the best of every other continent in a month-long tournament, hosted each time by a different country. Only a limited number of teams can qualify, and it is to Scotland's credit that such a small nation has reached the final rounds so often. Can it ever hope to beat the giants of soccer—teams like Brazil, Italy, Argentina and West Germany? Experience has shown that in every World Cup, a combination of chance and skilled leadership has propelled one or two teams from small countries into near-winning contention: Holland and Denmark are two recent examples. Scotland's turn may come. It is a team renowned for its unpredictability, and for a hard-to-define Scottish quality called *gallus*; a team with gallus is a feisty team, obstinate and somewhat reckless in the face of overwhelming odds.

Although soccer goes back a long way in Scotland, it shares its ancient pedigree with another popular sport, one thought to have originated in the country (although the Dutch also lay claim to having invented it).

In 1457, the Scottish King James II passed an act of Parliament aimed at preventing his subjects from frittering their time away when they should have been practicing their archery for future wars. He banned two sports. One was soccer. The other was golf—the game's first mention in any written record.

Less than fifty years later, in 1502, King James IV caught the craze, bought himself a set of clubs and began to drive and putt with his subjects. In 1744, a group of Leith golfers formed an association that became the world's first golf club. A few years later the spiritual home of world golf was created with the establishment of the Royal and Ancient Golf Club of St. Andrews. This is the body that today, in partnership with the United States Golf Association, sets the rules of the game.

Modern Scotland has more than four hundred golf courses, from the legendary St. Andrews (which all are allowed to play on, providing they can pay the fee and win a place through a daily lottery) to the challenging nine-hole courses of the Western Isles. There is a strong tradition in Scotland of golf being a game for all, without the artificial social barriers put up by insiders in some golfing regions of the world.

The third great sport of Scotland, and one that Americans would recognize as being similar to their version of football, is rugby. Common to its U.S. cousin is the oval ball, the physical contact, and the scoring by touching down the ball and kicking it over a goal crossbar.

Unlike soccer, rugby is a game for amateurs, even at the top level. It enjoys particularly strong support in the Lothian and Borders regions. Each year the Scottish national rugby team competes with teams from England, Wales, Ireland and France in the popular "Five Nations" tournament.

There are several ski slopes in Scotland, but they are not of a high standard, and fall well behind European rivals in off-trail facilities. The Scots who go skiing tend to be the kind who can afford the increasingly cheap option of jetting off to a mountain resort in Switzerland, France or Austria for a week or two.

If Wednesday evening means a trip to the floodlit soccer stadium for some Scots—kick-off seven thirty P.M.—the fact that it is October 31 means a very different night out for others.

Halloween is one of the two biggest traditional Scottish festivals. Essentially a celebration for children, it involves youngsters dressing up in fancy dress for an evening's "guising." Guisers go around in groups of two or three, knocking on people's doors. Instead of saying "trick or treat," the Scottish guisers are expected to perform a party piece—a song or a poem—before being rewarded with food or money.

The other essential part of Halloween is the Halloween party. The party location will be decked out with traditional emblems recalling the

Curling is popular in Scotland. Played here on a frozen loch at Dalmeny, the aim of the contest is to get the stone as close as possible to the center of a marked circle. The Scotsman Publications Ltd.

festival's origins—the days when the eve of All Saints' Day was thought to mark the height of supernatural activity. In place of the American pumpkin jack-o'-lantern, Scots scoop out the insides of large rutabagas to make "neep lanterns." Traditional games will be played—ducking for apples and eating treacle scones suspended from pieces of string, both played without using hands.

Christmas has become a major Scottish festival only recently. Historically the Kirk frowned on it as a pagan celebration, and it was not made a public holiday until 1967. Nowadays it is indistinguishable from the English or American Christmas, with decorated fir trees, carol singing and lavish exchanges of gifts.

Another Scottish festival heavily influenced by customs south of the border is Guy Fawkes Night, on November 5. It celebrates the discovery in 1605 of a plot to blow up the Houses of Parliament in London on the day the king was due to open them. The conspirators were caught, and a man named Guy Fawkes confessed under torture to being their leader. To commemorate the event, huge bonfires are lit the length and breadth of Britain and a crude effigy—the "guy"—is burned on top. If this sounds nasty, the celebration's uglier historical overtones have long been forgotten by most people, and the evening's real purpose is to give an opportunity for elaborate displays of fireworks.

The most important Scottish festival, however, is New Year and New Year's Eve (*Hogmanay*). Customarily Hogmanay begins with a meeting at a pub, followed either by a trek to some public place where a clock will chime the midnight hour or home to see the new year in with the family. This is one of the occasions when Scots reserve breaks down, with kisses and embraces shared equally among relatives, friends and strangers, and much singing of "Auld Lang Syne." After midnight, it is time for the traditional "first-footing," which involves visiting a friend's or relative's house with the aim of being the first foot over the door in the new year. Tradition demands the first-footer should be tall, dark and handsome—redheads are unlucky—and should be carrying a lump of coal. All being well, the host will be expecting company, and will have laid on ample supplies of food and drink, including shortbread and black bun.

Often the first-footer's destination is a party. Scottish New Year's parties tend to be long-drawn-out affairs, lasting for perhaps twenty-four hours after the bells chime the old year out. It is perhaps fortunate that Scots enjoy two days' public holiday after December 31, rather than one!

Along with these national festivals, there are numerous local celebrations linked to particular historical events and traditions. The most spectacular is the annual Shetland festival Up-Helly-Aa, in which Shetlanders celebrate their Viking origins. On the last Tuesday in January, a specially selected group of men called the "Jarl's squad," dressed in full Viking regalia of horned helmets, battleaxes, armor and capes, parade through the islands' capital, Lerwick. After nightfall the squad leads a torchlit procession of hundreds of costumed Shetlanders to the sea, where a beautiful replica of a Viking longship has been built. Gathering around the boat and singing, the members of the procession fling their torches at it. The longship is consumed in a breathtaking inferno. The rest of the night is spent in merrymaking in halls around the town.

One A.M.

Most Scots are asleep again, ready for another day. All but a few pubs and clubs have now closed; the Halloween guisers are tucked up into bed, the parties are over. Police from Scotland's eight regional police forces (there is no national police force in the U.K.) patrol the streets in their black uniforms and peaked caps with black-and-white checkered bands. Unlike their opposite numbers in most other countries, Scottish and other British police do not carry guns.

The last lights go out in tenements and tower blocks and terraces, leaving a land and seascape punctuated by the glow of city streetlamps, the flares of offshore oil installations and, on some nights, the strange phosphorescent curtain of the aurora borealis, suspended in the sky. To an astronaut looking down from orbit, the little specks of light that mark the human habitations of sleeping Scotland would seem at one with the rest of the dark half of the globe.

But modern Scotland does not in reality merge so simply with the wider world: This is because, more than anything, it is haunted by its younger self. Next must come a look back across a greater dimension, that of time—a look at Scotland's history.

CHAPTER VIII

Birth of a Nation

The Span of Time

In the churchyard of Fortingall, near Loch Tay in the southern Highlands, grows a withered tree. Legend has it that when the tree was still
only a thousand years old, a Roman named Pontius Pilate was born
nearby. That was about two thousand years ago, when Scotland first
entered written history. If the great-grandparents of a present-day teenage girl were born seventy-five years before she was, she would still
have to add about seventy-five "greats" to get back to her ancestors who
were alive at that time. And Scotland's story begins further back still,
much further back.

The Frozen North

The Ice Age ended, and Scotland emerged from its mantle of glaciers,
about 10,000 B.C. But some fifty centuries of gradual climactic change
passed before the first settlers arrived. These were small groups of

people who had no materials save stone and wood for tools. They dressed in furs and skins. They hunted wild animals for food, supplementing their diet with wild fruits and plants. After hundreds of years, these Stone Age people began to settle instead of roving from place to place in search of food. They set massive, unhewn slabs of rock upright in the ground, in precise circles, to mark their places of worship. They built "chambered cairns," rough domes of piled stones. By 2000 B.C. they had built settlements like that at Skara Brae in Orkney, with thick, strong walls of neatly shaped stone blocks. They even had stone furniture. Just as important, they were learning how to be farmers as well as hunters, growing crops such as barley and keeping cattle.

By about 1000 B.C., a new technology had reached Scotland, whose inhabitants had so far learned just one major scientific process, making fire. The new development was the creation of artificial metals.

First to come was bronze. Using this metal for their red swords and spearheads made the Bronze Age people the dominant culture until, between 300 B.C. and the birth of Jesus, a more technologically advanced race arrived on the scene with a tougher and more versatile metal: iron.

These settlers, or invaders, of the Iron Age were the Celts. Originally from Central Europe, they arrived in Scotland in successive waves, also spreading into Ireland, England and France. Along with iron, they brought to Scotland horses, war chariots, a well-developed religion based on a variety of gods, a new degree of sophistication in handling plow and livestock and a dramatic range of building techniques—most based on the need for self-defense in a violent age. They built mighty forts on hilltops, houses on stilts called *crannogs* in lochs and marshes, and the extraordinary *brochs.* More than five hundred *brochs* have been found in the far north of Scotland, some still in prime condition. They are towers, shaped like squat bottles over 60 ft. (18 m.) high, made of carefully stacked dry stone. Tiny entrances lead to passages within the

Key Events in Scottish History

Year	
81:	Romans invade Scotland.
400:	Last Romans gone.
843:	Kenneth McAlpin crowned first King of Picts and Scots.
1034:	Duncan becomes King of area similar to modern Scotland.
1072:	Switch from Celtic to Anglo-Norman Scotland begins.
1263:	Norwegian power in Scotland defeated at Battle of Largs.
1296:	England conquers Scotland.
1314:	Battle of Bannockburn: Scots beat English.
1328:	England recognizes Scottish independence.
1411:	First Scottish university, St. Andrews, founded.
1513:	James IV dies as Scots army beaten at Flodden.
1560:	Scottish Protestant rebels make pact with England; Catholic church in Scotland overthrown.
1603:	Union of the Crowns: Scotland and England under one head of state.
1638:	Scots rally round National Covenant.
1642:	English civil war.

immensely thick walls where—it is supposed—the inhabitants lived.

The Empire Strikes

Scotland's Celtic world got a major jolt in A.D. 81, when Roman troops marched north to conquer the country.

1651:	English troops occupy Scotland.
1660:	English leave.
1698:	Darien disaster.
1707:	Union of Parliaments: Scotland and England under one government.
1746:	Battle of Culloden: Jacobites defeated.
1778:	First Scottish cotton mill built.
1802:	World's first practical steamship launched in Scotland.
1888:	Scottish Labour Party formed.
1914–18:	First World War.
1918:	All Scotsmen and most Scotswomen get the vote.
1931:	Great Depression brings traditional Scottish industry to its knees.
1939–45:	Second World War.
1969:	Commercial quantities of oil first discovered in the North Sea.
1973:	Scotland, with the rest of the U.K., joins the European Community.
1979:	Scottish people vote in favor of limited autonomy; rejected on a technicality.

From their origins in Italy several hundred years earlier, the Romans had imposed their culture by force on a huge area of the ancient world. Their rule stretched from the Caspian Sea to Portugal, from Libya to the borders of present-day Germany. Unlike the tribal Celts, scattered across the wilderness in tiny villages and forts, the Romans had a highly ordered, technologically advanced society. They built durable, straight highways of stone, elegant buildings with tiled roofs and marbled floors, immense cities and open-air theaters. Many of them could read and write. They organized an efficient administration that could control their millions of citizens, subjects and slaves over vast distances. Their troops marched and maneuvered in tight formations against which the chaotic charges of the Celts broke in disorder.

The Romans had already conquered the Celts or "Britons" of the area that would become England when they attacked their Scottish counterparts (known to the Romans initially as Caledonians, then as Picts). Caledonia was not desired for itself by the Romans. As far as they were concerned, it was a dismal hell-hole, fit only for savages. But England

Reconstruction of a dwelling like those used by the Romano-British inhabitants of southwest Scotland in the first centuries after the birth of Jesus. The roof poles would have been thatched with reeds or turf.   Author

held promise as a colony, and the Romans did not want the Caledonians raiding their English property when their back was turned.

The Roman general Agricola speedily suppressed the Caledonians, beating them in a mighty battle at a place called Mons Graupius. The site of the battle is uncertain, but its name, misspelled by a medieval historian, survives in the name of the Grampian Mountains, which make up the eastern Highlands.

In a bid to consolidate their victory, the Romans built a chain of forts between the Forth and the Clyde, linked by roads. For a short time, south of this line, there existed a precarious form of the Romano-British lifestyle that had already sprung up in England.

Even as the empire reached this geographical peak of conquest, however, its downfall was beginning. Soft living and power struggles in the Roman homelands, together with attacks by warlike tribes on the northern and eastern borders, forced a withdrawal from the provinces. By about A.D. 100, the Romans had switched from attack to defense. Between A.D. 122 and 128, the Roman Emperor Hadrian built the great wall, which still stands today, bearing his name. Running from the Solway Firth to the River Tyne, where the modern city of Newcastle lies, it was 73 mi. (117 km.) long, 20 ft. (6 m.) high and thick enough for two men to walk abreast along the top. Impressive as it was, if its aim was to keep the Picts out, it did not work. Nor did the later Antonine Wall, a lesser structure of stone and turf running between the Forth and Clyde. By the end of the fourth century A.D., the Romans in Scotland were no more than a memory.

The Romans, armed with the learning of their predecessors, the Greeks, and with their own flair for organization and practical technology, were the first people to give Europe an idea of unity. Their language, Latin, remained the common tongue of European scholars and diplomats for centuries. We still use their alphabet. The briefness of

their stay in Scotland certainly contributed to the cultural divide between that country and England, which was exposed to Roman influence for much longer. That the Romans left their mark on Scotland at all meant a loose federation of small tribes had been offered a glimpse of a complex, rigidly ordered society.

The Unification of Scotland

The departure of the Romans left Scotland up for grabs for any of a number of migrating peoples—or for its existing inhabitants, if they could hold their own. The history of the unification of the nation spans more than six hundred years, a vast stretch of time over which the eyes of the historian are blinded by lack of written records. Hence the era's name, the "Dark Ages." What few scraps of information have been pieced together speak of treaties, royal marriages (a traditional way of uniting rival kingdoms) and, most of all, battles, although many of these would have involved no more than a few hundred men on each side. The rest—the peaceful years, the years of famine and disease, the songs and stories and festivals—we have to imagine for ourselves.

Initially there were four contenders for the prize of Scotland. Dominant for most of the era were the Picts, who carved out a powerful kingdom in the fertile lands of the northeast, shielded on one side by mountains, on another side by the Firth of Forth and on two sides by the sea. With their capital at Scone near Perth, they held sway over present-day Fife, Tayside, Grampian, Caithness, Shetland and Orkney. Though usually presumed to have been Celtic, their exact origins are shrouded in mystery. They left beautifully carved stones as memorials,

A carved Pictish stone slab, found in the extreme northeast of Scotland and dating from about A.D. 800. It shows a hunting scene; the upper figures are a horsewoman followed by two trumpeters. National Museums of Scotland

including one showing a group of warriors who bear an extraordinary resemblance to those of ancient Assyria—a culture removed by thousands of years and miles.

The Scots themselves landed in Scotland from northern Ireland about A.D. 500. Three brothers from the Irish kingdom of Dalriada set themselves up as rulers of Jura, Islay, Kintyre and the Oban area. The language they spoke is the precursor of modern Gaelic. They did not call themselves Scots, and we do not know where the name comes from, although it appears in Latin texts from about A.D. 400. It seems likely they were called Scots as a nickname by other Celtic peoples. Ironically, these incomers never knew Scotland as Scotland. The Gaelic word for the country was "Alba," and it still is.

South of the Scottish settlements lay the kingdom of Strathclyde, the last remnant of Romano-British society. Stretching from the Clyde to northern Wales, its people retained some of the order and discipline of the Romans, were skilled in the use of horses and lived in hilltop villages surrounded by stockades.

In the southeast of the country, nowadays covered by the Lothian and Borders regions, was the land of the Angles. This race had come to England ("Angle-land") along with another people, the Saxons, from the Baltic coast of mainland Europe as the Romans left, and set up a number of separate kingdoms. In about A.D. 600, they founded the kingdom of Northumbria, which at its most powerful stretched to the Firth of Forth and far into northern England. The Anglo-Saxon language is the root of modern English. Scots today still sometimes use the word *sassenach* to describe an English person, a word that stems from "Saxon."

The fifth people—the Norsemen or Vikings from Scandinavia—were relative latecomers. To the Scots, Christians by that time, they were the "Black Gentiles," from Denmark, and the "White Gentiles," from Norway. From the end of the eighth century to the thirteenth, they took

Shetland's Scandinavian past is celebrated in the annual ceremony of Up-Helly-Aa.
Scottish Tourist Board

over Orkney, Shetland, the Hebrides and the northern mainland.

In 685, the Picts won an important victory over the Northumbrians at Nechtansmere. Gradually, as a united people based on secure and fertile land, the Picts came to dominate the Scots as well.

Why, then, do the Picts disappear from history, and the Scots emerge as dominant? We cannot be sure. Some historians still hold the belief, accepted without question by Scotland until modern times, that the Scots destroyed the Picts in a great climactic battle. Nowadays a more common view is that a merger, forced perhaps, took place between two peoples already linked by blood ties and facing a common threat from northern enemies (the Norsemen) and southern enemies (strengthening Anglo-Saxon kingdoms, which were forming the ancestor of modern England).

Whatever the true story, what *is* known is that in 843, Kenneth McAlpin was crowned the first King of a united nation of Picts and Scots. (Some historians have a tidy theory that the Pictish crown passed from generation to generation down the female line, and that Kenneth simply married his way into the position of heir to the throne.)

Kenneth's realm stretched only as far south as the Forth-Clyde line. But in 1018, his descendant King Malcolm II beat an army of Anglo-Saxons at Carham to give Malcolm the kingdom of Lothian, the northerly part of old Northumbria. Malcolm was also able to install his grandson Duncan on the throne of Strathclyde. When Malcolm died in 1034, Duncan became King of a united Scotland whose borders were quite similar to those of the present day. Orkney, Shetland, the Western Isles and much of the Highlands still lay in the hands of the Vikings. But the strain of controlling their far-flung oceanic empire kept the bulk of mainland Scotland safe from their dreaded longboats and axes. From then on, Scotland faced only one military threat—England.

State of the Union

To imagine Scotland in 1034 is to force oneself to subtract many of the everyday items modern society takes for granted. There were no roads, scarcely any stone buildings, no electrical devices or machines of any kind. There was no medicine save magic, prayer and herbal remedies. There was no food except what communities could grow or hunt themselves. There was no written law, and only a tiny number of handwritten books. When night fell, there was no light but firelight or the dim glow of a resinous pine twig—except for candles in the homes of the wealthy. What little trade there was consisted of barter—Scotland had no coinage of its own until the twelfth century. Much of the country was covered with impenetrable forest, where wolves roamed, or bleak bog and moorland. For the ordinary folk of the villages, people living just a few miles away were foreigners to be regarded with deep suspicion, and a journey to another land might as well have been a visit to the moon.

These medieval Scots had a wealth of stories, songs and legends to tell each other around the fire during the dark evenings. They had their own unwritten traditions of justice, according to which a man had to pay for killing another according to the rank of the victim. The wealthy leaders, tribal chiefs called *mormaers*, lived in stout wooden houses lined with furs and skins and other trophies; but most of the people lived in humbler dwellings, huts of sticks, mud, turf and perhaps some stone.

The people were Christians. St. Ninian set up the country's first monastery on the Solway Firth at the end of the fourth century, and the Scots had already been converted to Christianity by the time they landed on the west coast. In 563, Scotland's most famous missionary—Columba—arrived from Ireland. A statesmanlike priest from an aristocratic family, his shrewdness was a great asset to the Scots as they clung to their new realm. Columba also made a dangerous journey into Pictland to try to convert the Picts. He set up an abbey on the tiny island of Iona, off Mull, the ruins of which remain to this day.

In 664, a meeting of clerics was called at Whitby in England to decide what form of Christianity Scotland should practice—the Celtic faith of Columba, where clergymen could marry, a faith of informal, independent priests; or the strict, centrally controlled religion of Roman Catholicism. The gathering came down in favor of Catholicism, and in 710 Nechtan, King of the Picts, was baptized as a Catholic Christian.

Legend tells of a stranger visiting the Pictish court during the Dark Ages, bearing a bundle of bones he claimed were the last remains of the apostle Andrew. The shrine the stranger built above the grave in

Fife grew into the cathedral town of St. Andrews, and Scotland got its patron saint.

The Normans Invade

In 1057, Malcolm III, named "Canmore" or "Bighead," became King of Scotland. His dynasty would last for more than 150 years and see a total change in the Scottish way of life.

Nine years after Malcolm ascended the throne, the Anglo-Saxon kingdom of England, under its ruler Harold, was conquered by invaders from France—the Normans, led by the clever and ruthless William. Malcolm married an Anglo-Saxon refugee from the invasion, Margaret. Malcolm himself had been brought up in the English court from the age of nine, and he and Margaret tried to bring the softer, more luxurious way of life of England's ruling class to Scotland. They shifted the center of power from the Celtic north to the Anglo-Saxon lands of Lothian, encouraged the Catholic church in preference to the still-lingering free-wheeling Celtic faith and spoke the Anglo-Saxon tongue—"Old Scots"—rather than Gaelic.

In 1071, William, tired of Scottish raids on England, invaded Scotland. The Scots were no match for his heavily armored cavalry and his powerful fleet. In 1072, Malcolm admitted defeat and performed the important ritual of homage to William—acknowledging him as his lord and master.

Scotland Becomes Anglo-Norman

The next eighty years saw the transformation of southern Scotland into a "feudal" society. After his death, Malcolm was replaced by a succession of three sons, each more Anglo-Norman in character than the one before. King David, the last, reigned for twenty-nine years; he was

Feudal Scotland

How did Celtic and Anglo-Norman feudal Scotland differ? In the original Celtic world, the king was no more than a chief of chiefs, accepted as military leader of a loose confederation of tribes. He could also expect certain services, such as hospitality, from each tribe. The tribe in turn was held together by ties of kinship: Members of it were part of an extended family, bound to obey their chief, the *mormaer*, as head of the household, father of all.

In the feudal world, society was based on a rigid pyramid of power, which in turn rested on the ownership of land. The feudal king was the ultimate owner of all land in his country. Everyone below him was a tenant. The first ranks of tenants were the great nobles, the lords, dukes and earls, who held sway over huge areas of land. A band of smaller landowners, the lairds, were tenants of the nobles. Below them were the great mass of people, the peasants or serfs, tilling tiny strips of land, grazing a few cattle, sheep and pigs.

The king granted land to the earls and lairds on the condition that they provide him with fighting men for his wars. Equipping the heavily armored cavalries that were crucial in battles of this era required great resources, which the earls and lairds extracted from their land at the expense of labor and goods from the peasants.

educated in England, where he had been a favorite companion of the English King Henry I. King David did more to introduce the feudal system to Scotland than any other monarch. He was a large landowner in England, and had no hesitation in handing over vast tracts of Scotland to his French-speaking Anglo-Norman friends.

With names that are still common in modern Scotland, such as Sinclair, Fraser, Lindsay, Crichton, Melville, Gordon, these incomers conscripted their new tenants as laborers, forcing them to build great timber towers and stockades—in some cases making them pile up immense artificial mounds of earth to build on. In time these "keeps" would be replaced by stone castles.

Not all the new feudal lords were Anglo-Norman. David and his descendants made many *mormaers* into nobles, and the rigid class distinctions that emerged in medieval England were tempered in Scotland by the lingering legacy of Celtic family ties.

The reign of David saw other important innovations. Many monasteries and abbeys were built, beautiful buildings lovingly crafted by masons capable of carving stone as if it were soft wood, decorated with pillars and arches and images of angels and monsters, the like of which the Scots had never seen before. The abbots became as rich and powerful as the greatest earls, their monks tilling fertile fields and gardens, their libraries precious storehouses of written knowledge (this was before printing existed in the West), their cellars overflowing with wine and ale for thirsty travelers, their chapels decorated with gold and silver and tapestries. David also whipped the church as a whole into shape, establishing bishops and seeing the first cathedrals built.

Alongside the establishment of a royal mint to make Scotland's first coins, David also founded the first "burghs," little townships of merchants and craftsmen that had a monopoly on trade. Usually based on a single street lined with a semifortified terrace of houses, these royal burghs became magnets for tough, ruthless traders who would come to wield great economic and political power. Many of the traders were English, and the new Scots language, derived from the mixture of Anglo-Saxon and Norman French they used, became the language of commerce. This was one of the reasons Gaelic gradually died out as the speech of Lowland Scotland.

David's fourth innovation involved overhauling, and in many cases creating, the machinery of government itself. His brother Alexander, who was King before him, had already appointed royal officers to look after finance, the army and written records. David went further and established a Royal Council to advise him on policy. This council would one day grow into the Scottish Parliament. "Justiciars" and sheriffs were created, too, to judge legal matters when the King was absent.

All this meant that by the time David died in 1153, Scotland was emerging as a more organized nation; a powerful minority of its citizens were enjoying more prosperity; and its rulers were better able to hold their heads up as equals in the courts of their richer European neighbor states.

But the changes applied only to southern and eastern Scotland. In the Highlands and Islands, the old Celtic lifestyle was as strong as ever, and many thousands of people still owed allegiance to the King of Norway.

A Tale of Two Treaties

In 1165, following the death of the last Scottish king to hold a Celtic name—Malcolm IV—the warlike William ascended the throne. He was known as "the Lion" after the design of his emblem, a red lion on a yellow background. The emblem became the Scottish royal flag, a rallying point in battle ever since (alongside the Scottish national flag, the X-shaped white "St. Andrew's Cross" on a blue background, displayed on the back of this book's jacket).

Scotland's border with England was not yet fixed, and William claimed the old kingdom of Northumbria as his own. At first he hoped to persuade England's King Henry II—who ruled over it—to hand it

Scotland's Parliament

Medieval parliaments were the distant precursors of modern democratic assemblies like Congress and the parliaments of twentieth-century Europe. Their introduction marked the first suggestion that the rule of a hereditary king and his court (a collection of the king's friends, relatives, advisers and staff) could be challenged by an alternative authority. At this thirteenth-century stage, however, the Scottish Parliament's members were not democratically elected. They were drawn from the ranks of major landowners and bishops. In its earliest form, Parliament was a kind of Supreme Court. Many centuries would pass before it won the right to make laws and govern the country.

over peacefully. He helped Henry in his wars with France to encourage him. This policy failed, and in 1174, William invaded England.

The Scottish army got as far as Alnwick, about twenty miles south of the modern border, before it was beaten by the English. William was captured and sent into exile in France. There he was obliged to sign the Treaty of Falaise, in which he accepted Henry as his lord and master. Henry sent troops to ravage southern Scotland in revenge for William's impudence, and garrisoned its major castles.

The Treaty of Falaise was not the first time Scottish kings had humbled themselves before English monarchs. But unlike those previous occasions, this one left absolutely no doubt about what it meant: All Scotland was Henry's feudal territory, and all Scots were his "vassals"—his tenants, in feudal terms.

For most of the seventy-two years after William's death in 1214, there was peace with England. In 1237, a conference settled the exact position of the border. Alexander II (1214–1249) and Alexander III (1249–1286) were able to build on the work of David. From this era dates the development of the Scottish Parliament. The burghs prospered, as did the monasteries and abbeys. Yet most people still lived off the land in conditions of great poverty.

The age of the Alexanders was one of simmering revolt and endless raids by Celtic nobles on Lowland Scotland. A still bigger problem was the continuing Norwegian presence in the Hebrides. When Alexander III tried to dislodge the Norwegians from the Western Isles with a series of raids, it provoked a violent response. In 1263, Norway's aging King Haakon organized a massive fleet, which would have numbered perhaps two hundred ships carrying fifteen thousand men. But the once-great seafarers had not counted on the ferocity of the autumn storms. Haakon's fleet was torn apart by gales before it could assemble. By the time the remnants made landfall at Largs on the Clyde approaches, they were so weakened that the Scots beat them easily. In 1266, by the Treaty of Perth, Norway gave up all its Scottish possessions save Orkney and Shetland in exchange for a cash payment.

Twenty years later, as he hurried through the darkness from Edinburgh (by then Scotland's capital) to meet his new wife, Yolette, Alexander III could look back with some satisfaction on the achievements of the Canmore dynasty: half a century of peace with England, an increasingly united and prosperous Scotland; the future held promise. It was not to be. Alexander's horse slipped as he passed the cliff at Kinghorn, Fife, and the king plunged to his death. A new and terrible chapter in Scotland's history was about to begin.

The Struggle for Independence

Hammer of the Scots

Alexander's three children had already died, and the crown passed to his only heir—his baby granddaughter, Margaret, who was in Norway. The ruler of England at this time was Edward I, one of the most fearsome adversaries Scotland would ever have to face. A tall, powerful, learned man, he had a ruthless, innovative mind, which he used to great effect in the fields of war and politics. He would become known by the Latin nickname "Scotorum Malleus," the Hammer of the Scots.

Edward immediately set about arranging for his son to marry the infant Margaret. He had just spent ten weary years fighting to add Wales to his kingdom, and though he wanted Scotland, too, he would have preferred to win it through the time-honored method of a royal marriage. The Scots nobles running the country agreed to the marriage,

Dingwall ●   ● Elgin

Inverness ● □ *Culloden*
                1746

Harlaw ○
1411
(Battles Against the Clans)

● *Aberdeen*

● Fort William

Forfar ●   ● *Montrose*
Dundee ●   *Arbroath*
Scone ●
Perth ●   St. Andrews ●
Abernethy ●

IONA

Stirling Bridge 1297 ✱
● Stirling

Bannockburn 1314 ✱
✱   Edinburgh   ● Dunbar
Dumbarton ●
Glasgow ●   Linlithgow ●   □ Haddington ●
○ *Largs*   *Falkirk*   *Prestonpans*   ● Berwick
1263   *1298*   *1745*
✱ *Loudon Hill*   Roxburgh ●   ○ *Flodden*
● Ayr   *1307*   Jedburgh ●   *1513*

MAJOR BATTLES

✱ *Wars of Independence*
  (1296–1314)
□ *Jacobite Rebellions*
  (1707–1746)
○ *Other Battles*
● **Historic Sites**

Dumfries ●

Kirkcudbright ●

E N G L A N D

but little Margaret died on the way back from Norway to Scotland. The crisis deepened when, in the absence of a definite heir, thirteen candidates put themselves forward for the Scottish crown.

It seems strange to us that the man asked to choose which of the thirteen should receive the crown was Edward himself. But at this stage, many of Scotland's Anglo-Norman nobles still had estates in England, and did not think of themselves as Scottish. Besides, in the rigid class structure of those days, aristocrats felt it took one man at the top of the feudal pyramid, a king, to recognize another such man.

Edward chose John Balliol, a sixth-generation descendant of David the First. His choice was motivated by the knowledge that John (later nicknamed Toom Tabbard, "empty coat," by the Scots) was a foolish, easily dominated character. Edward made it clear that he regarded himself as overlord of Scotland, and summoned the timid John to London on the slightest trivial matter.

Scots impatience with John grew, and in 1295, a council of nobles persuaded him to refuse an English demand for money. Soon afterward Scotland made its first treaty with England's archenemy, France—a friendship that became known as the Auld (Old) Alliance.

Edward wasted no time in replying. In 1296, he led his army of veteran troops north, sacked the rich Scottish border town of Berwick, slaughtered hundreds of its citizens, beat the Scottish army at Dunbar and went on to take the main castles and burghs in the south of the country. Toom Tabbard surrendered and was sent into exile. Edward shipped the sacred slab Scotland's kings were crowned on, the Stone of Destiny, back to London, along with much of the nation's archives, and made hundreds of Scots sign a pledge of loyalty to him.

The ruins of thirteenth-century Sweetheart Abbey, near Dumfries, stand testimony to the skill of its builders, and the destructiveness of both war with England and the Protestant Reformation. Author

Scotland was a defeated nation, garrisoned by foreign troops, on the verge, it seemed, of complete subjection to English rule. But the country had fight in it yet.

Wars of Independence: Wallace

Scotland faced formidable military disadvantages compared with England. It had only a fifth of its opponent's total population. It was far poorer. Its most fertile land, and its centers of power and wealth, were within a day's march of the border, whereas the equivalent areas of England lay far to the south. Edward had also discovered a deadly weapon during his Welsh campaign, the longbow, with which relatively small units of archers could slay troops at a distance in great numbers.

Despite all this, and despite many supposedly Scottish nobles having fought alongside their English friends in the campaign of 1296, revolt broke out. It was encouraged by the unpopularity of the general Edward appointed to rule Scotland in his absence, John de Warenne, Earl of Surrey. Warenne and the greedy English officials beneath him showed themselves as contemptuous of the Scots as was King Edward, who called them "filth."

The sporadic revolts that erupted in the remoter parts of Scotland soon found their rallying point in William Wallace, son of a minor laird. In 1297, he killed the English sheriff of Clydesdale and found himself leading a band of rebel Scots. At the same time, in the north, an army of Gaels was gathering under the leadership of Andrew De Moray. The two forces linked up after several successful sieges and skirmishes to face the might of the English at Stirling.

In battle, the medieval Scots typically formed themselves into several large divisions of spearmen called *schiltrons*. In defense, the *schiltrons* would be tight circles, impregnable to cavalry, bristling with spearpoints like porcupines. For attack, they were less effective, finding it hard to maneuver as a group.

But fancy maneuvers were not needed this time. The two armies faced each other across the River Forth. Spanning the river was a narrow wooden bridge. The impatient English knights lumbered across the bridge two or three abreast, and on the Scottish side their heavy horses became entangled in a bog. The Scots spearmen bore down on them and slaughtered them with ease. Many English nobles died. A ramshackle rebel army had beaten the mighty English war machine.

Soon the Scots were raiding the north of England with all the brutality and greed for plunder the English had shown them the year before. Wallace meanwhile took the reins of power as Guardian in the name of the exiled Toom Tabbard. His glory was to prove short-lived.

In 1298, an enraged Edward returned to Scotland. His army, ill supplied and mutinous, was not the force of two years before. But Wallace and his army of common folk and small landowners were betrayed by the Scottish nobles. They were the only group that could provide the cavalry Wallace needed to protect his *schiltrons* from English foot soldiers, but the nobles stood aloof, despising him and his commanders as social inferiors. When the clash came at Falkirk, the *schiltrons* repelled the first reckless charge of the English knights. Then Edward brought up his archers. The deadly arrows rained down from the sky on the tightly packed ranks of spearmen, slaying them by the hundreds and opening the way for a fresh cavalry charge which routed the Scots.

Wallace escaped. He was captured in 1305 and tried by the English as a traitor. He was dragged through the streets of London, hanged, drawn, hideously mutilated and pulled into quarters. His head was stuck on a spike by London Bridge, and the four parts of his body were publicly displayed in Newcastle and in three Scottish towns. His was just one cruel death among many of the Wars of Independence, some due to Wallace himself. But the execution shows the deeply divided nature of medieval society across all borders—had Wallace been a noble, he probably would have been imprisoned or ransomed in exchange for a cash payment. It also shows the increasing bitterness and hatred between the English and the Scots, a bitterness that helped form each country's sense of national identity.

Wars of Independence: Bruce

It is an all too common mistake in history to put national success or failure down to a single individual. But in Robert Bruce the Scots would find, at a critical moment, a man capable by his leadership alone of swinging the odds in their favor.

Bruce's first steps on the path to glory did not bode well. In contrast to Wallace, he was an earl, from one of Scotland's leading Anglo-Norman families. His grandfather had been one of the thirteen contenders for the Scottish throne after the death of Alexander III. Bruce was motivated in early adulthood by a passionate belief in his right to the crown, and was prepared to do anything to get it. He was a liar and a traitor, having changed sides several times during the first years of the Wars of Independence, one moment forming a band of rebels to fight the English, the next swearing loyalty to Edward and attacking his fellow Scots.

In 1306, Bruce arranged a meeting at a Dumfries church with a fellow claimant to the throne, John Comyn. The meeting ended with Bruce murdering his rival. Whether this was a calculated action on Bruce's part or the hot-tempered conclusion to a history of mutual hatred between the two is not known. But Bruce now faced charges of murder and sacrilege, having killed a man on holy ground. The Pope excommunicated him, meaning he was excluded from any kind of religious ceremony (a particularly grave penalty in those days, when the Church so dominated daily life). Bruce decided his only chance to escape worse punishment and perpetual exclusion from the race for the crown was to seize the throne immediately. He hurried to Scone and, with the help of powerful friends and relatives to lend the occasion some credibility, was crowned King.

At once the fledgling monarch was on the run. Although Scotland seethed with revolt in the open country between the English-garrisoned castles, it was too disorganized for Bruce to lead. Besides, to many Scots he was a murderous upstart, a former ally of the English and quite untrustworthy. In June of 1306, the English routed his tiny army near Perth and executed every man except the priests.

Between 1306 and 1307, the fugitive Bruce hid in the wilderness of the north and southwest, planning his comeback. This came with a vengeance when, in May 1307, he trounced the English at Loudon Hill.

Two months later, King Edward died peacefully while with his army as they marched toward the border. The English throne passed to Edward's namesake son, but Edward II was a poor general. After leading the English army unsuccessfully into Galloway, he turned for home.

The next seven years saw Bruce gradually build up his following in Scotland and capture the English-held strongholds. As his skills as a commander and his personal magnetism became evident, he began to win the loyalty of ordinary Scots. The period may also have seen a transformation of his own character from an opportunistic, self-seeking Anglo-Norman into something approaching a Scottish patriot.

With Edward paralyzed by dissent at home in England, Bruce succeeded through a mixture of guile and guerilla tactics in capturing Forfar, Brechin, Dundee, Perth and Dumfries. Between campaigns in Scotland he raided England, giving the English a taste of the suffering they had inflicted on his own country.

In 1313, the English-held stronghold of Linlithgow was captured by

A modern painting of the Battle of Bannockburn. The small knot of horsemen in the center of the picture is Robert Bruce and his commanders. Beyond them can be seen the Scottish pikemen pressing forward against the last remaining English resistance. The dark mass of troops in the distance, heading for the trees, is King Edward and his retreating army.
Stirling District Council

Bruce's men after they wedged a haycart under the raised iron gate at the entrance to the castle. Armed men leaped out from under the hay and dealt with the defenders. Next year the mighty fortress on Edinburgh's Castle Rock fell when Thomas Randolph led a small unit of soldiers up a secret path to the summit. Only Stirling Castle now remained in English hands. Edward marched north in early summer 1314 to relieve it. A pitched battle was inevitable.

The two armies met at Bannockburn, a few miles south of Stirling. With about fifteen thousand foot soldiers and two to three thousand armored cavalry, England had mustered its most powerful force ever. Scotland was outnumbered three to one.

The Battle of Bannockburn opened on Midsummer's Day with an unplanned single combat. An impatient English knight galloping ahead of the rest of the army was felled by Bruce with a single blow of his axe. Two full-scale English charges were then repulsed by the steadfast *schiltrons.* The next day the Scots advanced on the English, who had made their camp in a swampy neck of land between the burn and the river Forth. The Scots halted to take the impact of the first English charge, which failed, and marched on. The English were trapped: Their infantry could not attack because their cavalry was in the way, and their cavalry had no room to charge and had to fight on foot. Before long Edward's army broke, and the men were slaughtered or captured. Although Edward escaped, he had suffered a hideous defeat. Scotland's independence was won.

Declaration of Independence

The war continued; Edward and Bruce raided each other's countries more than once before they died. But these were the aftershocks of a political earthquake that had reached its peak with Bannockburn. All that remained was for Bruce to be recognized as King of an independent Scotland by England and the rest of Europe—including the Vatican, which still regarded Bruce as a sacrilegious murderer.

In 1320, the Scottish nobles and clergy wrote to the Pope pleading for his support to reach a just peace with England. Their letter, which became known as the Declaration of Arbroath, was more than a mere request: It was a statement of independence by an emerging nation, coming at a time when the idea of patriotism was first forming as an alternative to the existing calls on loyalties from family, God and feudal master. It said:

As long as 100 of us remain alive, we will never in any way be forced to tolerate the rule of the English. Because we do not fight for glory, or riches, or honors, but for freedom alone, which no good man gives up except with his life.

In 1328, by the Treaty of Northampton, England finally recognized Bruce and the independent nation of Scotland. In the same year the Pope agreed to absolve Bruce of his sins. When Bruce died in 1329, his work was done, the nation of Scotland well founded and secure. In the centuries that followed, the foundations would be tested to destruction.

Divided Kingdom

Bruce's death left a yawning gap at the top of Scotland's barely formed government that would take many decades to fill. Through the fourteenth and fifteenth centuries his successors had to struggle to impose order on an anarchic, quarrelsome, deeply divided society. Bruce had held out to future generations the ideal of a nation. But giving that ideal form and reality, planting in the minds of Scots a common respect for a centrally imposed system of law and order as we understand it today, was a huge task.

It was a task also faced by Europe's other emergent states as the continent made the slow transition from the medieval to the modern age. National rulers everywhere faced similar problems of carrying out and enforcing their policies when outlying communities in even small kingdoms might be many days' travel away, when powerful nobles were

A Lifetime Guarantee

Here is an example of a Bond of Manrent, a formal agreement between a commoner and a noble by which the commoner became part of the noble's household. For Patrick Chene of Essilmount—provided his lord is just—the bond is a mixture of a job for life, a guaranteed homestead, a pension plan and personal protection in an age when only vagrants, peddlers and outlaws could go it alone. As for the Earl of Erroll, the bond with Patrick gives him a new tenant to farm his land and a new name to add to his roll of fighting men. The document, dating from 1516, is translated from the original Scots. It is accompanied by an extract from the Earl's half of the bargain, the Bond of Maintenance.

Bond of Manrent

Be it known to all men by these present letters I, Patrick Chene of Essilmount, to be bound and obliged, and by these my letters and the faith and truth in my body bind and oblige me and become man, to a

accustomed to running their territories like miniature states of their own, when commerce was a clumsy operation running along slow, dangerous trade routes and when only a handful of people could read and write.

Scotland being a poor country on the edge of Europe, covered with moor, forest and mountains, its problems were especially great. Scottish nobles, many of them still virtually tribal chieftains, would not lightly give up their traditions of proud personal independence in the face of royal demands. They gathered around them great private armies of

noble and potent lord William, Earl of Erroll, Lord Hay and Constable of Scotland, and to his male heirs gotten of his body, they being of 19 years of age, that I shall be loyal, true and faithful to him and to them . . . because my said good lord and master has enfeifed me in his lands of Tawarty for all the days of my life for my service foresaid. To the observing, keeping and fulfilling hereof I bind and oblige me to my said lord and master in the surest form of obligation without fraud and guile. And these my letters to endure for all the days of my life.

Bond of Maintenance

Be it known to all men by these present letters we William, Earl of Erroll, Lord Hay and Constable of Scotland, to be bound and obliged, and by these our letters and the faith and truth in our body strictly bind and oblige us, to our loved cousin Patrick Chene of Essilmount, forasmuchas he is become special man to us and our male heirs . . . herefore we bind and oblige us . . . that we shall supply, maintain and defend the said Patrick in all and sundry his righteous causes and quarrels moved and to be moved.

followers, bound to them by feudal obligations, by kinship and, toward the end of the era, by formal "bonds of manrent." What money the king managed to raise in taxes would barely support the civil service, standing army and legal system he needed. Scotland faced the constant menace of a large, aggressive neighboring state, England, without the comfort of potential allies close at hand. And it was Scotland's misfortune to find itself saddled time and time again with an infant monarch who was too young to rule, leaving the nobles to squabble over who should govern the country until the King came of age.

The fourteenth century in particular marked hard times and suffering for the Scots. Any national unity built up during the Wars of Independence collapsed with the death of Bruce and the experienced leaders who had fought alongside him. England overran Scotland once more, and was expelled only after years of bitter fighting, which saw some fickle Scottish nobles change allegiance to support the old enemy. The Black Death took its grim toll. A disastrous succession of kings took the helm. There was Bruce's son David, who came to the throne aged five and spent much of his subsequent reign as a contented prisoner of the English, only winning release at the expense to Scotland of a crippling ransom. There was Robert Stewart, first of the Stewart dynasty, who failed dismally to live up to his early promise as a brilliant military commander. And there was his disabled son, also named Robert, who virtually abandoned the throne in 1399, creating a particularly long and bitter factional struggle among the nobility. Small wonder that one chronicler wrote at the time:

. . . there was no law in Scotland; but the great man oppressed the poor man and the whole country was one den of thieves. Slaughters, robberies, fire-raising and other crimes went unpunished, and justice was sent into banishment, beyond the kingdom's bounds. [Translated from the original Scots.]

As the fifteenth century wore on, however, the tide began to turn. One of the chief reasons for this was a great series of wars between England and France, which for several decades drew English military power away from Scotland. Another threat to the crown, from the powerful Lords of the Isles, was beaten back by force of arms in 1411. The ruling lord, Donald MacDonald (*Mac* means "son of"), and his army of Gaelic-speaking Highlanders were forced to withdraw from the prosperous northeast of Scotland after a bloody battle at Harlaw near Aberdeen.

Then, in 1424, a new Scottish king came of age: James I. He was to rule for just twelve years before being assassinated, but in that short

The Black Death

*This evil led to a strange and unwonted kind of death. . . . the sick
. . . dragged out their earthly life for barely two days. . . . Men
shrank from it so much that, through fear of contagion, sons, fleeing as
from the face of leprosy or from an adder, durst not go and see their
parents in the throes of death. [Translated from the original Scots.]*

The words of the chronicler John of Fordun, who experienced the
terrible impact of the Black Death at first hand in the
mid-fourteenth century. The highly infectious, flea-borne plague is
thought to have killed a third of all Europeans, and the Scots were
not spared. It left profound social changes in its wake, most
importantly a shortage of labor, which led to a loosening of feudal
ties between peasant and laird or noble. Peasants began giving their
landlords money instead of goods or services, making them less like
slaves and more like free, rent-paying tenants as we understand
today.

time he brought a new level of order and stability to the turbulent
nation. His stated aim was to make "the key keep the castle, and the
bracken-bush the cow"—in other words, to rein in the private armies
and bandits who threatened all life and property and made a mockery
of the law.

King James, the first of seven to bear the name, pushed legislation
through Scotland's Parliament (still a weak body when faced with a
strong monarch) on a vast range of subjects, from the extermination of
wolves to soccer. He overhauled the nation's fragile financial system.
He set up semipermanent courts to hear complaints and pass judge-

ments. He backed up this peaceful activity with ruthless suppression of rebellion. Two of his first, most straightforward laws, here translated from the original Scots, leave no doubt that he meant business:

Item that firm and sure peace be kept and held through all the realm and among all and sundry lieges and subjects of our sovereign lord the King. And that no man take on hand in time to come to cause or make war against others under all pain that may follow by course of common law.

Item it is statute and ordained that no man openly or notoriously rebel against the King's person under the pain of forfeiture of life, lands and goods.

James I, "wise, valiant and a good justiciar" as one French visitor described him, was betrayed and murdered in Perth in 1437. His heir, James II, was yet another boy-king. This was the pattern in late medieval Scotland: two steps forward, one step back as the power of the Crown against the nobility ebbed and flowed.

The experiences of James II with the Douglas family demonstrate the bitterness and violence of the conflict. The Douglases had always been a thorn in the side of the Stewarts. From their power base in the Borders, they grew strong from endless feuds with similar families in the north of England. By the end of the fourteenth century, the Earl of Douglas ruled lands from Galloway to the Moray Firth, and could muster thousands of fighting men.

Other powerful nobles became just as fearful and suspicious of the Douglases as were the Stewart kings. The turning point came in 1440, with James II on the throne. He was nine years old. The country was being ruled in his name by Sir William Crichton, who invited the young Earl of Douglas and his brother to dinner at Edinburgh Castle. With the young king present, Sir William had the Douglases beheaded. Twelve years later it was James himself who dealt the killing blow. Luring the new Earl of Douglas to Stirling Castle with promises of safe conduct, he stabbed him to death and launched a rapid, successful campaign against the victim's outraged followers. James escaped punishment for his action. It seemed most Scots accepted the murder as the legal execution of a mutinous subject.

The Renaissance Finds Its Man

The close of the fifteenth century and the dawn of the sixteenth saw a fresh wind blowing through Europe's musty medieval ways. It was the time of the Renaissance, the rebirth of forgotten Greek learning and the birth of new wisdom. Columbus showed the way to America—to the Europeans, a new world. Magellan proved Columbus's theory that the world was a globe by sailing around it. Brilliant Italian artists like Leonardo da Vinci and Raphael broke out of the confines of traditional painting to work wonders with perspective and chiaroscuro, the means by which figures and scenes on a flat surface appear three dimensional. The political theorist Machiavelli put forward a ruthless, pragmatic idea of leadership that held a ruler was entitled to put the interests of his country before any kind of morality.

For the first time since the death of Bruce, Scotland found itself with exactly the right man at exactly the right moment in history. That man was King James IV, who came to the throne in 1488. He was a model Renaissance ruler: well-read, a linguist, with a keen interest in technology, determined to make law and trade work smoothly, and ruthless in putting the well-being of his nation before that of individuals. In the twenty-five years of his reign, Scotland became a more prosperous, cultured, well-organized society. Two hundred years after Bannockburn, the country seemed about to secure for itself an independent voice and a distinctive character amid the heaving turmoil of emerging European nation-states.

James was able to build on the achievements of his predecessors and to take advantage of various favorable circumstances. Scotland's first university, St Andrews, had been operating since 1411, to be joined forty years later by a second at Glasgow, providing a pool of learned, literate men. The merchants and craftsmen who controlled the trading burghs had managed to keep themselves apart from the strife between kings and nobles, and had been quietly prospering. The nobles for their part were increasingly ready to air their grievances in law courts or in Parliament, or to the King directly, rather than settling matters with a battle. And the long peace with England was holding.

Scotland remained poor in comparison with the rest of Europe, and even among the nobles and merchants there were few with money or inclination to encourage the arts and sciences. But James IV's reign saw the founding of a medical college in Edinburgh (1505); the setting up of the country's first printing press (1507); and a law that required all landowners to send their eldest sons to school or university. Architecture began to be more decorative, and less based purely on the need for defense. Castles at Linlithgow, Falkland and Craigmillar became expensive royal palaces. Scotland's first great poets appeared, writing in a language that could have formed the basis for a modern Scottish tongue.

James improved Scotland's fledgling legal system, making court sessions more regular and calling wayward sheriffs to heel. To the astonishment of his courtiers, he learned Gaelic and tried to persuade the Highland chiefs to control their clans. When the talking failed, he turned to force and, though he never subdued the Highlanders, managed to keep them away from the Lowlands.

James turned his attention to every sphere of life. When he was not courting women, he would be discussing with an alchemist how to turn base metals into gold, or inspecting new artillery at his Edinburgh gunworks, or sponsoring a bold clergyman's experiment with human flight. (The cleric in question, an abbott, jumped off the ramparts of Stirling Castle with a pair of homemade wings strapped to his arms. He plummeted earthward and broke his leg. He blamed this on having used chicken feathers instead of those of more airworthy birds.)

Life in the Scotland of James IV is documented by a wealth of eyewitness or near-contemporary accounts, the most famous being that of a Spanish envoy, Don Pedro de Ayala, who sent detailed reports of the country back to Spain. This dispatch dates from 1498:

The people are handsome. They like foreigners so much that they dispute with one another as to who shall have and treat a foreigner in his house. They are vain and ostentatious by nature. They spend all they have to keep up appearances. They are as well dressed as it is possible for such a country as that in which they live. They are courageous, strong, quick, and agile. They are envious to excess. . . .

The kingdom is very old and very noble . . . not rich; the fault of which is not owing to the land. But on the other hand they are not so poor but that they live as well as others who are much richer; only they have nothing to put into their strongboxes.

Another account, Scottish this time, describes King James's love of jousting tournaments:

. . . at sundrie tymis he wald mak proclamatiounis throw the land, to all and sundrie his lordis and baronis quha were abill for justing and turney, to cum to Edinburgh to him, and their exercise thaimselfis for his plesour; sum to rin with the speir, sum to fecht with the battell-aix, sum with the two-handit sword and sum with the hand-bow and uthir exercisis. Quhasaevir focht best got his adversariis wepoun deliverit to him be the King, and quha ran best with the speir got ane speir headit with pure gold deliverit to him. . . . The King brocht the realm to greit manheid and honouris; that the fame of his justing and tourney spread throw all Europe. . . .

[. . . At sundry times he would make proclamations through the land, to all and sundry his lords and barons who were able for jousting and tourney, to come to Edinburgh to him, and there exercise themselves for his pleasure; some to run with the spear, some to fight with the battle-axe, some with the two-handed sword and some with the hand-bow and other exercises. Whoever fought best got his adversary's weapon delivered to him by the King, and who ran best with the spear got a spear headed with pure gold delivered to him. . . . The King brought the realm to great manhood and honors; that the fame of his jousting and tourney spread through all Europe. . . .]

Toward the end of his reign James was able to devote more time to foreign affairs. He dreamed of putting his growing navy at the head of a crusade by Christian Europe against the Turkish Empire. But despite Scotland's heightened European status, his main diplomatic role was limited to a delicate balancing act between the old enemy, England, and the old ally, France.

He lost his balance in 1513. England had a new ruler, Henry VIII, every bit as brilliant as James and much more aggressive, with all the power of a wealthy, populous trading nation behind him. Henry had joined an alliance with three of the most powerful rulers of Europe with the intention of smashing France. He knew James would want to help France, Scotland's traditional ally. Sure enough, the Scottish king answered French calls for aid and marched across the border into England with his country's last and biggest feudal army, perhaps twenty thousand men. The English force that met them at Flodden in the Cheviot Hills was of about the same size. The two sides pounded each other with artillery, then advanced to close quarters.

Too late the Scots foot soldiers, armed with their traditional long spears, discovered the English had an unfamiliar weapon, the bill-hook. Fitted with an axe blade and cruel, curving spikes, it could lop off a spearhead before killing an opponent at close quarters. The Scots, fanatically loyal to James and suicidally brave, stood their ground. At least ten thousand died, the King among them. It was Scotland's worst military defeat, marking the end of the country's hard-won confidence in itself and in the long-term security of its independence. Within forty-five years of Flodden a mass movement of Scots, borne on a wave of religious fervor, would take the first fateful steps toward giving that independence away.

The head of a bill-hook like those used by English troops at the Battle of Flodden. The Board of Trustees of the Royal Armouries

Enter the Kirk, Exit the King

The Catholics Fall from Grace

The established religion in medieval Scotland was Roman Catholicism. Save for a small Jewish community, there was no other. So it was across the whole of Europe: millions of people, speaking many tongues, all worshipping God according to the practices laid down by an immense hierarchy of priests, bishops and cardinals, answerable in turn to the single Holy Father, the Pope in Rome. All heard the same Latin words spoken at masses, marriages and funerals.

In Scotland, as everywhere in Europe, the Church was far more than a ceremonial organization that baptized people, married them, buried them, blessed them and forgave them their sins. The Scottish peasants knew it as one of the "thrie estatis" (three estates) that ruled their lives, the other two being the nobles and the leading citizens of the burghs.

The Church carried news in the unlettered, preprinting days, issuing from the altar messages, warnings and exhortations to its flock from beyond the congregations' limited horizons. It was the chief patron of music and architecture, with its churches, cathedrals and abbeys the most beautiful and substantial buildings anywhere in Europe. Only the Church possessed libraries, and the resources to copy books by hand; only the Church had large numbers of people who could read, write and count. Churchmen thus performed most of Scotland's clerical, academic, legal and administrative tasks. The Church was a substantial landowner. It expected and received ample reward—financial and material—to sustain itself. The Scottish people sought in return at least the possibility of divine protection from war, plague, famine and more everyday setbacks, plus the certain prospect, after a hard, weary life, of a place in Heaven.

How did the Catholic Church so alienate itself from the Scots that this whole structure came crashing down? There were many reasons, but essentially it was a case of an institution already rotting from within clashing with a society going through a fundamental transformation.

The rotting process meant that the Scottish Catholic Church did not live up to its own rules, and did not provide what its congregations demanded. More and more senior Church posts were filled by people who had no religious training—nobles and royal relatives who simply wanted the income that went with the job. As a result, parish churches fell into disrepair and what few parish priests remained had to do extra jobs or squeeze money from their congregations to survive. Many of them were illiterate and ignorant of their duties. Priests were supposed to be celibate; by the beginning of the sixteenth century many were openly taking mistresses and fathering children.

At the same time the Scots themselves were changing. Merchants and nobles were becoming as wealthy, learned and literate as the clergy. The advent of printing broke the Church's monopoly on the reproduction of the written word. As the questioning spirit of the Renaissance filtered through to the ordinary Scottish people, they began to ask themselves why even conscientious priests spoke the word of God to them in Latin—a language they did not understand—and not in their own tongue. Why could they not read the Bible for themselves? Why, some began to wonder, were the rules of worship rigidly laid down by a group of men hundreds of miles away in Italy?

Although the Catholic Church in Scotland was crumbling fast of its own accord, it was in Germany that the first successful alternative to Catholicism took root. In 1517, in Wittenberg, Martin Luther outlined a new ideal of worship, which became known as Protestantism. He believed that people earned Heavenly forgiveness for their sins through their individual faith in God, not through a priestly ceremony. He urged a return to the teachings of the Bible and the abolition of what he saw as the unnecessary frills of Catholicism—elaborate ritual, ornately decorated churches, overpaid clergymen living in luxury. The shock waves of this "Reformation" spread rapidly outward. Europe's nation-states either switched to the new religion or stuck with Catholicism, which began its own radical reform program. To the fervor of the masses was added the calculating control of powerful rulers.

The conflict soon spread to England and Scotland. Printing presses, now widespread, unleashed a flood of propaganda. English translations of the Bible, previously available only in Latin, were smuggled into Scotland, and the first Scottish Protestants were publicly burned to death by the Catholic authorities. Then, in the 1540's, the new strife of Catholic versus Protestant awakened the slumbering specter of a more ancient feud.

England's King Henry VIII, who had beaten the Scots at Flodden in

1513, was by this time a kind of semi-Protestant. To suit his own ends, he had seized the lands and properties of English monasteries, renounced the authority of the Pope and set himself up as head of a new "Anglican" (English) church. He was thus in the unique position of being his country's military, political and religious leader.

Scotland meanwhile was in turmoil. Protestantism was gaining ground in the burghs, among the nobles and among the peasants. In 1542, the Scottish crown passed to a baby girl, Mary. But real control of the country lay in the hands of Mary's mother, Marie de Guise, a staunch Catholic and a native of France.

Scotland thus became caught up in the Reformation power struggle. On one side stood Marie de Guise, her Scottish supporters, the Catholic Church and Catholic France. On the other stood the Scottish Protestants—still an underground movement at this stage—and King Henry, who wanted Scotland for himself. Henry tried to realize his ambition with a marriage treaty between his son and the infant Scottish Queen Mary. But that fell through; and the English king decided he would have to win Mary's hand by force.

The invasion he unleashed on southern Scotland in 1544 was the most brutal and destructive the country had ever seen. The English army swept resistance aside and did its utmost to follow its grim orders:

. . . Put all to fire and sword, burn Edinburgh town, so razed and defaced when you have sacked and gotten what you can of it as there may remain forever a perpetual memory of the vengeance of God. . . . Do what you can out of hand and without long tarrying to beat down and subvert it and all the rest, putting man, woman and child to fire and sword without exception, where any resistance shall be made. . . .

Had Henry held back, Scotland's growing number of Protestants might have forced through an alliance with England by themselves. As it was, Henry's "rough wooing" sent Scotland temporarily into the hands of supporters of France and Catholicism. The infant Queen Mary was sent to France where, in 1558, she married the heir to the French throne. Back in Scotland, once the English withdrew, Marie de Guise continued to rule in Mary's place, filling the court and the corridors of power with Frenchmen.

Triumph of the Protestants

But storm clouds were gathering for Marie and the French in Scotland. In 1557, a group of Protestant nobles met to sign the Covenant, an agreement pledging to fight the Catholic establishment, which they called the Congregation of Satan. Their motives were political (they resented French influence) and financial (they eyed Church wealth) as much as religious, but they made the Protestants a power to be reckoned with and forced Marie to act.

Scotland's many poor people were also growing restless, using the new Protestant doctrine to back up their long-standing resentment of church wealth. This "Beggars' Summons," directed at friars who grew fat off charitable donations intended for the poor, was posted at the doors of friaries throughout all Scotland in 1559:

. . . you have, by your false doctrine and wresting of God's word (learned of your father Satan), induced the whole people, high and low, in sure hope and belief, that to clothe, feed . . . and nourish you, is the only most acceptable alms allowed before God; and to give one penny, or one piece of bread once in the week is enough for us. [Translated from the original Scots.]

In the same year, the smouldering nation was inflamed by the return to Scotland of the preacher John Knox, an expert propagandist, skilled in the art of whipping up congregations to a frenzy. His Protestantism

IOANNES CNOXVS.

Woodcut believed to be of John Knox. Scottish National Portrait Gallery

was not the moderate Lutheran creed of the early Reformation, but the uncompromising Calvinist variety. This held that everyone except a number of "elect" believers, chosen by God before they were born, was destined to suffer eternal torment in hell after death. Calvinists saw virtually all Catholic rituals and festivals as blasphemy and called for a Church answerable to no authority but its own and God's.

Riots flared in Perth after Knox preached there, soon followed by other outbreaks of violence across southern Scotland during which monasteries were torn down, altars smashed and religious statues and pictures destroyed. In this heady air of revolution, a popular Protestant host made up of people from every level of society marched on St. Andrews and Edinburgh. Marie de Guise appealed for French help, and got it, but the Protestant Scots found an ally, too.

That ally was the country's oldest enemy. In 1560, one of the crucial turning points in Scotland's history, the Scots put five centuries of conflict aside and made a bond with England, a bond that would lead directly to the unification of the two kingdoms.

A new monarch had just ascended the English throne—Queen Elizabeth, a Protestant. Reluctant as she was to deal with the volatile Knox, the chance to complete the religious transformation of her neighbor state and deal a much-needed blow to France proved irresistible. An English fleet cut the supply lines of Marie's French allies, and an Anglo-Scottish army laid siege to their base in Leith, the port of Edinburgh. Before long Marie was dead, and a treaty arranged for all French and English troops to withdraw from the country.

Parliament met and, in the name of the nation's absent Catholic Queen, abolished the Catholic Church. The saying of mass was forbidden, on pain of death. The new Church of Scotland, known as "the Kirk," was built on principles devised by Knox. It would be governed not by pope or monarch but by priests, meeting each year in a "general assembly." Knox also dreamed of a radical program of education for all and social security for the needy, although it would be centuries after his death before even the first of these became reality.

The Hottest Seat in Europe

In the same momentous year, Queen Mary's husband died and her position in France became difficult. Besides, her Scots subjects expected her back. In 1561, aged eighteen, she returned to a country she had not seen since she was a baby, to take up one of the hottest seats in Europe: the throne of Scotland.

Scotland remained central to the countless plots being drawn up by Europe's rulers at this time as the Reformation and the Catholic Counter-Reformation rumbled on. The people and Parliament of Scotland were determined, in the majority, to remain Protestant. Mary for her part refused to renounce her Catholic faith. Had she done so, she could—as the granddaughter of Henry VIII's sister—have inherited the English throne when Elizabeth died. Had she taken the other extreme, and launched a Catholic crusade with French or Spanish help against the Kirk, it could have seriously threatened the future of Protestantism in the British Isles. In fact she tried to steer a middle course. Confrontation was inevitable.

For months the widowed Mary delayed her choice of a new husband in the face of any number of European suitors. In the end she opted for Lord Darnley, a teenage Catholic noble whose good looks were matched only by his stupidity. The marriage sparked off a revolt by Protestant nobles, stamped out after the Queen herself donned arms and armor to lead loyal followers against them.

In 1565, less than twelve months after the wedding, the jealous Darnley and a group of thugs murdered pregnant Mary's Italian secre-

tary, Riccio, before her eyes. Darnley soon met a similar fate. In 1567, the Queen sent him to a house in Kirk O'Field, near Edinburgh, to recover from an illness. As he lay there, sick, he was strangled. The murderers then blew up the house with gunpowder. Eight weeks later Mary was married again, this time to James Hepburn, Earl of Bothwell.

That Bothwell was Protestant did not save Mary from a roar of popular anger. To Knox's moralistic Scotland, already scandalized by the Queen's celebration of mass, her bright dresses, the music and dancing that could be heard at night coming from the royal palace of Holyroodhouse in Edinburgh, this hurried marriage of two assumed conspirators in Darnley's murder was the last outrage.

Mary was taken from her supporters by a Protestant army, led through the streets of Edinburgh in a red petticoat to the jeers of the people and forced to abdicate. Her son was crowned as James VI, and Mary was imprisoned on an island in Loch Leven. In 1568, she escaped and, after a failed attempt to regain the crown, fled recklessly into England. Queen Elizabeth could not permit such a threat to her own throne to remain free, and imprisoned her. Mary was locked up until 1587, when Elizabeth ordered that her head be chopped off.

Two Crowns Become One

The majority of Scottish and English people were now Protestant. This new common ground prompted fresh thoughts on how stronger links might be forged across the border.

Back in 1544, with the pall of burning and butchery by Henry VIII's English troops hanging over Scotland, the idea that the two countries could be peacefully united would have seemed ludicrous. But four

Mary Stewart in royal mourning white. Painted by unknown artist after François Clouet.
Scottish National Portrait Gallery

decades later the picture had become very different.

King James VI took over the running of Scotland in 1583. He was only seventeen. But the notion that his destiny could lead him to become the first ruler of a United Kingdom of Scotland and England was already strong within him.

Events worked in his favor. The English ruler, Queen Elizabeth, had no heir. James had the family pedigree to make a legitimate claim to the throne. Elizabeth's powerful secretary, Robert Cecil, supported his bid; for while Scots were unpopular in England, Cecil knew a Scottish king could soon be absorbed into the rich court society of London and made to put English interests first.

To qualify for the English crown, James had not only to please the English but to keep the rest of Europe from rejecting him. He was a Protestant. He married a Protestant princess, dealt severely with Scottish nobles found to be plotting with European Catholic states and, just before Spain's unsuccessful attempt to invade England, signed a mutual defense treaty with Elizabeth. He sent no more than a formal protest to London when his mother was executed. But he strove at the same time never to do anything that would deeply antagonize the powerful Catholic rulers of southern Europe.

His balancing act was successful. Early in 1603, Elizabeth died, naming James her heir. On March 29, the Scottish people began hearing the news in a royal proclamation read out from marketplaces around the country. This revelation of their King's vision of unity must have stunned Scots, still only just getting used to the unfamiliar notion of

King James VI of Scotland, King James I of Great Britain. Described by the King of France as "the wisest fool in Christendom," he numbered among his achievements the sponsorship of the Authorized Version of the Bible and the authorship of the first antismoking tract, "A Counterblaste to Tobacco" (1604). But he alienated many of his Scottish subjects. Her Majesty Queen Elizabeth

a nonhostile England. James called for his people to have a "loving and kindlie dispositioun" toward their new English fellow citizens:

. . . that they represent and acknowledge them as their dearest brethren and friends, and the inhabitants of both his realms to obliterate and remove out of their minds all and whatsoever quarrels, grievances, or debates which have maintained discord or distraction of affection among them in time past, and with a universal unanimity of hearts join themselves as one nation, under His Majesty's authority. . . . [Translated from the original Scots.]

King James rode south with his court, full of anticipation at the prospect of the power and splendor awaiting him. He was not disappointed. On July 25, he was crowned James I, King of Great Britain, in London's Westminster Abbey. Hundreds of richly costumed nobles and clergymen thronged the building as drums and trumpets sounded in the streets and ships discharged their cannon across the River Thames.

For England, it was the start of a momentous reign, during which playwright William Shakespeare produced some of his greatest works, the first seeds sprouted of revolt against royal authority, and the foundations for an overseas empire were laid.

But for Scotland, the Union of the Crowns was a mixed blessing. The heart of its government and much of its cultural life was torn out when the king and his courtiers went away. From Scotland's point of view, the Union of the Crowns did not so much represent the arrival of Scotland on a wider stage; it mean rather the disappearance of a golden caravan of wealth and power over the horizon into a foreign and distant place.

CHAPTER XII

Joining Forces

A Scotsman, an Irishman, an American

Despite the Union of the Crowns, Scotland remained an independent country, and would do so for more than a century after King James's Westminster coronation. The King was now head of state of all Britain, but Scotland and England kept their separate Parliaments and separate government officials in Edinburgh and London. (It was as if the United States were divided into two parts, each with its own Congress and its own federal agencies, but under a single President.)

How then did this arrangement come to an end? How did Scotland arrive at a situation where its own Parliament negotiated itself out of existence? The sequence of events is a complex, interwoven one, but two of the most important factors underlying it were the divided loyalties of the Scottish people and the increasing opportunities for emigration overseas.

To take emigration first: Until about the time of the Union of the Crowns, there had been little more than a trickle of Scots settling abroad. These had been mainly soldiers of fortune marrying local women and raising families after military campaigns in mainland Europe. The rest of the Scottish people were effectively boxed into a geographical corner. If the English pressured them, they had nowhere else to go: They were obliged to stand and fight.

With the Union came a sudden new opening. Even as King James was riding south, the last stronghold of resistance to England's attempts to conquer Ireland fell. The Irishmen of Ulster, the northern part of Ireland, surrendered. The new King of Great Britain found himself ruler of all Ireland, too.

Up until this time, the English monarchs had tried to keep the Scots out of Ireland, which they wanted as a colony for themselves. To a degree they succeeded, although there were strong, ancient ties between the native Irish and the Gaels of the Highlands and Islands of Scotland.

Now all at once everything changed. A Scottish King was in charge. He had subjects to please, hungry for land and wealth, in both Scotland and England. He had a newly conquered territory, which needed to be secured if the natives were not to overrun it. What better way to solve the problem than to set aside most of Ulster for Scottish and English colonists?

So the Ulster Plantations were begun. (Most people nowadays think of the word "plantation" only in connection with tobacco and bananas, but at that time, it also meant a plantation of people.) To the Scots and English of the period, there were many similarities between the first colonies in Ulster and those in America. Not least of these was the treatment of the Irish, who were regarded, like Amerinds, as ignorant savages and suffered accordingly at the hands of the generally contemptuous incomers.

Scots began to pour into Ulster. Between 1608 and 1618, the early years of the Plantations, as many as forty thousand are thought to have made the short sea crossing to Ireland, setting the pace for the decades to come. Like many emigrants to America during the same period, a large number of those who left Scotland for northern Ireland were fleeing religious persecution at home. For although King James had initially been careful to pay lip service to the strict rule of the Calvinist Protestant Scottish Kirk, he started turning against it, as did his successors, trying to bring it under direct royal control like the more moderate English Protestant Church. Ulster began to fill with Scots who wanted to worship God according to their own strict creed, without elaborate ranks of priests and authoritarian kings telling them what to do.

In the end, many of these Ulster settlers found their new home was not far enough away from London to escape royal interference. Reluctantly, spurred on by landlord troubles, they packed up and crossed a wider sea to America, where they became known as the Scotch-Irish. They settled in the Appalachian Mountains, in Pennsylvania, in Virginia, in the Carolinas and in Georgia. An estimated quarter of a million of them had arrived by the dawn of the American Revolution. George Washington said if he was defeated everywhere else, he would make his last stand among the Scotch-Irish of his native Virginia.

It is impossible to know the degree to which emigration robbed Scotland of its will or ability to cling to independence in the seventeenth century. But there can be no doubt that the courage, vision and sense of purpose required to uproot a family and lead it to an unknown future overseas marked most emigrants as people Scotland could ill afford to lose.

A Question of Leadership

The conflict of loyalties faced by Scots who remained in their native land after the Union of the Crowns was a tough one. A people wishing to preserve its own identity needs leadership, but where was Scotland to look for that?

There was the King in London. James VI and his successors were descendants of the ancient Scottish house of Stewart, and the Scots on the whole saw them as right and proper heirs to the throne of Scotland. Provided they ruled fairly, they would be accepted as absentee heads

A recent painting by William Hole depicts the scene in Greyfriars Churchyard in 1638, when Scots gathered to sign the National Covenant. City of Edinburgh Museums and Art Galleries

of state. But the Stewart kings in England became increasingly arrogant and dictatorial, and continually clashed with the fiercely independent Scottish Kirk.

There was the Kirk itself. Most Scots supported its existence as the church they had chosen and fought for, and were prepared to go on fighting to resist any attempts to dismantle it. But right from its Reformation birth pangs, the people were divided over how radical the Kirk should be. Some felt it should have complete control over the nation's affairs: government by an assembly of elected priests, receiving guidance from God. At the other extreme, some were content to see the Kirk confine itself to conducting the country's worship.

Finally there was Parliament, that semirepresentative assembly chosen from the ranks of wealthy burgh citizens, clergy, nobles and, increasingly, small landowners or lairds. But the Scottish Parliament did not, for most of the seventeenth century, begin to look like the foundation for an independent government, a legislative body that would defy priests and the King's minions to rule by itself on behalf of the people. When it defied the King, it was to defend the Kirk; when it passed laws to weaken the Kirk, it was to please the King.

The Cost of Victory

The heightening tension between King and Kirk erupted into violence in 1637. On the throne was King Charles I, James's son. Like his father, Charles wanted the Kirk under his direct control. To this end he authorized a new prayer book for the Kirk that was so close to the English Anglican style that congregations rioted when they heard it, flinging chairs, sticks and stones at the luckless ministers in the pulpits. One bishop so feared violence from his flock that he preached with a pair of loaded pistols in front of him.

Charles insisted the new book be accepted. The Scots responded in

1638 with nothing less than a revolution. Nobles, merchants and senior clergymen met at Greyfriars Church in Edinburgh to sign the National Covenant, pledging to defend the Kirk. Later the document was sent around the country, and thousands more signed. Scotland was swept by a wave of religious enthusiasm that temporarily united both radical and moderate supporters of the Kirk in opposition to the king's wishes.

The Kirk's General Assembly and Parliament set up a joint administration, ignoring royal protests. A new Scottish army was formed under the command of the experienced general Alexander Leslie.

Charles naturally looked to his English subjects to raise money and troops to crush the rebellious Scots. But his reign was highly unpopular in England, too. His main opponent there was the English Parliament, which was far ahead of its Scottish equivalent in seeking the power to govern the country without royal or religious interference.

Soon bloody civil war broke out in England. Some rallied to the King, forming the Royalist army. Others joined a new force raised by the English Parliament. In 1643, the Scottish government and the English Parliament formed an alliance against the Royalists. The result was that by 1645 the Royalists were soundly beaten. Charles took refuge with the Scottish army, but refused to accept their terms; accordingly they handed him over to the English and marched home to Scotland, where the Kirk's power seemed stronger than ever.

Almost immediately the division of opinion among the Scots over who or what they were fighting for resurfaced. They had been united against their Stewart King in defense of the Kirk; but now that Charles had been taught a lesson, and the Kirk was secure, opinion swung toward negotiations to get him back on the throne.

The English, under the control of a self-styled "Lord Protector"— army commander Oliver Cromwell—would have none of this. Brushing aside Scottish demands, and defeating a Scottish military attack, he ordered Charles's execution. In January 1649, the second Scots-born

The Rule of the Kirk

To the Kirk radicals, every word of the Bible was literal truth. Most forms of pleasure were sinful, the work of the Devil. Plays, dancing, carol singing, bonfires, celebrations of Easter and Christmas—all were banned. Any form of work or play on Sundays was forbidden. In 1656, one Kirk session formally punished children for playing on Sunday. Serious offenses against the Kirk's moral code— especially adultery and premarital sex—attracted harsh penalties, or, at the very least, public humiliation by the local minister in front of the congregation. None of this helped make Scotland a more moral nation: It simply made people more secretive about their pleasures, and made them pretend they were living more "respectable" lives than they really were. This sense of guilt about having a good time is something the Scots have never quite succeeded in shaking off.

Stewart King of Britain was beheaded.

Even the most radical Scottish Kirk supporters were outraged by this. But their attempts to defy the determined and extremely able Cromwell were in vain. In 1651, the last Scottish army to fight the English under Scottish government orders was defeated at Worcester in England. Scotland had to suffer an eight-year occupation until the Lord Protector died.

Naively, at Cromwell's death, the Scots welcomed the news that another Stewart King, Charles II, was to take up the vacant throne of Britain. Even now few Scots realized the fundamental truth, that the Stewart monarchs in London, whose authority they could not bring themselves to renounce, would never accept a Scottish church that governed itself. Sure enough, Charles soon displayed the loathing of his ancestors for the Kirk.

The years that followed plunged Scottish society into deep disarray. Thousands of disenchanted Scots emigrated to Ulster. Many moderate Scottish worshipers accepted the King's changes to the Kirk, such as the reintroduction of bishops. Meanwhile the most radical Calvinist Protestants—the Covenanters—were forced to worship in secret, often in the open air. The government, now firmly backing the King, took harsh measures against them.

In 1666, out of one hundred prisoners captured after an uprising by Covenanter Galloway peasants, one third were hanged, two persons after torture. The rest were transported as slave labor to English plantations in the Caribbean. Congregations at the illegal open-air services began to arm themselves. The spiraling cycle of violence culminated in the "killing times" of the 1680's, when fanatical Covenanters would be shot on the spot by government troops if they refused to renounce their beliefs.

The whole sorry mess was finally brought to an end in 1689. Charles II had been succeeded by his son James, who was a Catholic. After three years the English had decided they could not accept a Catholic on the throne and had invited the Dutch Protestant William of Orange and his wife Mary (both of Stewart descent) to become joint rulers, sending James into exile. Scotland also accepted this; William and Mary in turn abolished the bishops and gave the Kirk its independence. It had taken almost 130 years and thousands of lives, but Scottish Protestants had finally won the right to decide for themselves what place God and religion had in their lives.

The price of the struggle was measured not only in death, destruction and emigration, but in the degree to which it distracted Scots from making provision to safeguard their political and economic independence. Attention now focused on the Scottish Parliament. Could it run the country in Scotland's best interests? Alas, its most ambitious step would contribute directly to its downfall.

American Adventures

If the sixteenth century was the Age of Discovery, when European nations ventured into the deep oceans and came across continents they had never dreamed existed, the seventeenth century was the Age of Colonization. Aggressive trading nations such as Spain, France, Holland and England set about ruthlessly exploiting the natural resources and native labor of new lands as they founded colonies across the globe, earning enormous wealth in the process.

So far Scotland had only dipped its toe into these risky but potentially rewarding waters, with minor or temporary settlements in Canada (hence Nova Scotia, New Scotland), New Jersey and South Carolina. Most Scots emigrants had settled in areas controlled by the English government, such as Ulster. But in the 1690's, a much bigger project caught the public imagination. The Scottish Parliament passed an act setting up The Company of Scotland Trading to Africa and the Indies. The company's plan was to set up a Scottish colony on the Isthmus of Darien, in present-day Panama. Its founders' dream was that goods and profits from trade between the Atlantic and Pacific would pour through the colony, and Scots rushed to invest in it. In 1698, three ships left Leith with twelve hundred colonists on board, under the leadership of Dumfriesshire visionary William Paterson.

All the signs pointed to disaster long before they set out. Money for the venture had been raised entirely in Scotland after King William, under pressure from the rival English East India Company, scared off English investors: The money represented half the impoverished nation's entire cash resources. Darien, dubbed New Caledonia by the hopeful settlers, was claimed by Spain. And the whole area, half jungle, half swamp, was a steamy tropical hell-hole, with insects and disease waiting to kill off the pale northern visitors.

Paterson and his followers stayed on in the little stockade they had built, Fort St. Andrew, for just nine months before heading for home. A quarter of the settlers had died of fever. The rest faced starvation, and the English colony in Jamaica would not help. By a horrendous piece of timing, two more expeditions had already set out from Scotland. The first came and left with the first wave of sickness. The second arrived just in time to be attacked by the Spanish and sent packing after valiant but futile resistance.

Thousands had died. Financially, Scotland was ruined. The Scots blamed England for the disaster.

The Last Act of Parliament

It was clear to everyone on both sides of the border that something in the relationship between Scotland and England had to change. The Darien fiasco showed Scotland how, under existing conditions, it would be all too easy for the English, jealous of local competition, to freeze Scottish merchants out of international commerce. As one bitter Scots pamphleteer put it in 1699, writing with unconscious irony in the London English that had become his country's literary language, his people were

. . . in a worse condition than any foreigners with relation to England: for if a foreign people discover anything that may be of advantage to them, they are at liberty to pursue it by themselves, or take in the assistance of others: and if they find themselves aggrieved by England, they have their respective Governments to make an application for redress. But we are the most unhappy people in the world, for if England oppose us, we have no King to appeal to, but one that is either an alien or an enemy to us, as being King of a greater people who are such: or if he be King of Scots, he is a prisoner in England, and cannot do it. . . .

England for its part feared that on the death of Queen Anne, King William's Protestant successor, the Scots would sever all links with England by appointing their own Stewart king, possibly a Catholic.

By the start of the eighteenth century, the arguments were more clearly defined. Although as late as 1705 all-out war between the two countries seemed possible, 1706 found Scots and English sitting around the conference table. Debates in the Scottish Parliament raged between those who wanted to maintain the existing union of dual governments, but with a fairer deal on trade, and those who backed the English idea of a single London-based Parliament and administration.

Belatedly, men like Andrew Fletcher of Saltoun began to speak out against the way the English pulled the strings in the Scottish Parliament. He had his supporters, and when the terms of the proposed Treaty of Union became known, many ordinary Scots were angered to see that it was based on the single-Parliament scheme. Riots broke out in Edinburgh, Glasgow and Dumfries, and troops maneuvered edgily on either side of the border. The English government, unsure of having enough Scots politicians in its pocket, sent secret agents north. Soldiers protected the supporters of Union from the fury of the mob as they made their way to and from Parliament House in Edinburgh.

But, predictably, opposition was divided. In January 1707, members of Parliament approved the Act of Union by 110 votes to 69. The independent Scottish government was no more. Complaints that supporters of the new Union of Parliaments had been encouraged by the promise of handsome payments and cushy jobs were in vain. From now on the Scots would be ruled wholly by London, where Scottish representatives made up less than a tenth of the members of the new British Parliament. "There's ane end," commented a Scots politician at the time, "of ane auld sang." (An end of an old song.)

The Fall
of the Clans

State of the Union II

Scotland in 1707 was a country of some one million people, about a fifth of its present-day population. The majority still worked the land for a living. They lived in scattered hamlets, growing barley to brew drink and oats for food. Oatmeal was eaten as porridge or as a hard baked biscuit. Cattle, sheep and goats were kept for food and clothing. Outside the castles of the great nobles, the ordinary folk lived in houses of unmortared stone, thatched with turf over rough wooden roof beams. Smoke from the fire escaped through an opening in the roof, and if there was any other opening besides the doorway, it was unlikely to be a glass-paned window. Floors were bare ground; furnishings and utensils were sparse. Communities were linked by rough tracks or paths. Even the best roads would become impassable to wheeled vehicles in winter.

Centuries of tree felling had led, outside the Highlands, to an almost completely deforested landscape.

By 1707, Scotland had several hundred burghs. These ranged in size from towns like Edinburgh, Glasgow, Dundee and Aberdeen, all with more than ten thousand inhabitants, down to tiny villages with under a hundred. In the larger burghs, houses and workshops were densely packed together in a crazy jumble of alleyways ("closes" or "wynds"), where fire and disease were constant threats. On the whole the burghs were not very sanitary: The stench of Edinburgh was legendary, not surprising in a city where householders would yell a warning of "gardy loo!" (from the French *gardez l'eau,* "mind the water") before hurling the day's waste matter out the window. From these towns a growing class of wealthy merchants traded with all the ports of northern Europe. Ships set sail for the continent with wool, linen, corn, herring or coal, and returned laden with luxuries like wine or silk, manufactured goods, and raw materials hard to obtain in Scotland.

The merchants, arrogantly proud of their status at the top of the burgh's social ladder, and of the fact that they dined on white bread and wine rather than oatmeal and ale, preferred to form close-knit guilds rather than compete tooth and nail for trade. They were not adventurous when it came to opening up new markets overseas. But their contacts with Europe made the towns increasingly cosmopolitan, outward-looking places. In Edinburgh's High Street, merchants rubbed shoulders with skilled craftsmen such as silversmiths (silversmithing was a craft in which the Scots excelled); with lairds from the countryside; with bands of bearded Highlanders, swords and pistols slung from their belts; with lawyers, students, ministers of the Kirk, beggars, peddlers, laborers.

This is how Scotland stood at the moment of the formation of the United Kingdom and Parliament of Great Britain. But what Scotland?

Questions of Dress

The relationship among the plaid, the kilt and the woven woollen cloth of colored check pattern known as tartan is uncertain and the subject of constant debate. The plaid spread throughout the Highlands during the seventeenth century. At some point this single sheet of material divided into a lower skirt part and an upper part; the lower part evolved into the modern kilt. It has been suggested the kilt was actually invented in the early eighteenth century by an Englishman.

The earliest pictures of kilts date from the 1740's, and they seem to have been most popular among Scottish nobles, clan chiefs and military officers who supported the Jacobite (King James II) cause. After the battle of Culloden in 1746, the government banned the wearing of plaids and kilts by everyone except regular Scottish soldiers. Thanks to the British army's desire to standardize regimental uniforms, the plaid died out. The army style of kilt, a knee-length pleated skirt with a pouch—*sporran*—hung in front of it, became the norm that would be copied when civilians were

Only the English-speaking part. The Gaelic Highlands remained untamed. The last battle was yet to come.

The King over the Water

In 1707, the Highlands were as hard as ever to control from Edinburgh or London. About a quarter of a million people lived beyond the boundary dividing Highlands and Lowlands, a line running roughly from Inverness to Glasgow via Braemar and Dunkeld. The people of the clans

allowed to wear it again.

The same story applies to tartan. The origins of the word are not known, but it was in use as early as 1500 to describe the brightly colored Highland fabrics of striped or checkered pattern. There does not seem to have been any concept of a "clan tartan"—it was a question of what material, and indeed what dyes, were available in the various parts of the Highlands. But certainly by the time of the Jacobite rebellions, many of Prince Charles's clan troops were dressed in tartan cloth.

As with the plaid and the kilt, the British army standardized tartan, devising a set pattern for each regiment. This notion of specific tartans associated with specific regimental names spilled over into civilian life, with the result that today some books claim to be able to cross-reference an exhaustive list of Scottish names with an equally large selection of "correct" tartans. Tartans are undoubtedly a very attractive range of patterns, but there is really no reason to wear anything other than the tartan that suits the wearer, rather than the tartan that supposedly suits the person's name.

were tough and fiercely independent, owing loyalty to kin and chief before any greater lord. The women worked hard at weaving, spinning, grinding meal and tending little plots of land while the menfolk looked after their cattle, hunted and fought feuds with other clans. They lived in rough dwellings even cruder than those of the Lowlands, though the chiefs were often well-traveled, well-educated men, with castles to rival those of southern Scotland. Gaelic was still their language. The women wore simple dresses and shawls. The men wore clothes that were even more straightforward; their costume was the plaid: a large rectangular piece of material that formed a skirt around the waist, and a folded band across the chest and back.

The Highlanders had for centuries seen little difference between the English and Lowlanders. They looked on them equally as soft, cowardly town dwellers. The English and the English-speaking Scots had just as much contempt for the Gaels, whom they thought of as idle, vicious savages. Every so often a clan or confederation of allied clans would emerge from the glens to ravage and plunder Lowland homes; the English-speaking Scots would seek to subdue them with shows of force.

Ultimately the old tribal way of life of the Highland clans fell victim to the juggernaut of modern progress. When the clan warriors left their mountain fastnesses for the final confrontation with the Lowland Scots and the English, they walked into a new Europe ruled by highly developed, centralized national governments, a Europe policed by tightly drilled, highly organized armies, a Europe of increasingly sophisticated manufacturing economies and all-embracing written laws. As the Amerinds, Australian Aborigines and Africans were beginning to discover, there was no place in the world of these new Europeans for a society of independent tribes. There was no respect, save sentimental regard, for oral literature, unwritten laws and the economics of barter. Unlike the native peoples of other continents the Europeans would colonize, however, the Highlanders lived close to this emerging modern world. For the clans, time had simply stood still while the world beyond the mountains changed out of recognition.

The years leading up to the Union of Parliaments saw the terms set for the final struggle. Scotland's conversion to the Protestant faith had as little impact on the Highlanders as Edinburgh law had. The Gaels never broke their historic ties with France and Ireland, as the rest of Scotland did. At the very time the Lowland Covenanters were forging links with the English Parliament, some clans began to rally around the

Stewart kings who had always opposed them. No doubt the Stewarts promised the clan chiefs handsome rewards if they helped in the struggle for the British throne. But Highland backing for the Stewarts also reflected the divisions between the clans. Past governments had never hesitated to use clan feuds for their own ends, issuing "letters of fire and sword" to enable one clan legally to exterminate another.

The most important split between the clans was that between the MacDonalds and the Campbells. From the pinnacle of their power as Lords of the Isles, the MacDonalds—based in Skye and the Outer Hebrides—were beaten back through the sixteenth and seventeenth centuries. At the same time the Campbells of Argyll were growing to wield more and more influence, becoming allies of the Edinburgh and London governments. The Campbells followed the Kirk as English-speaking Scotland did—their chief, the Earl of Argyll, was one of the most important figures in the Scottish Parliament—and they were generally glad to protect the Lowlands as a buffer against the wilder northern Gaels.

The enmity between these two very different kinds of Highlander came to a head in 1692 with a hideous crime that became known as the Massacre of Glen Coe. Many of the clans remained loyal to the exiled James II, the "King over the Water" in France; they and their supporters elsewhere in Scotland and northern England were known as Jacobites, from the Latin for James—"Jacobus." King William and his advisers decided that the Highlands must be brought under control. An order was sent out that all clan chiefs must take an oath of allegiance to William. The head of one small branch of the MacDonald clan, who lived in Glen Coe, was late in swearing his oath. Two companies of Campbell soldiers were given secret orders to kill every male member of the clan under the age of seventy. The Campbells arrived in the glen and asked the unsuspecting MacDonalds for hospitality, which they received and enjoyed for several days before turning on their hosts and slaughtering thirty-eight of them—including two women and two children. The survivors fled into the snow-covered mountains, where more died of exposure.

The massacre was one of many incidents that encouraged the Jacobites to try to take advantage of general Scottish unhappiness in the first few decades of the Union. The English felt they had "bought the Scots, and the right to tax them." Seeking cash for a war with France, for instance, the English-dominated British Parliament had no hesitation in passing tax laws discriminating against Scotland's vital linen industry. In spite of this treatment, the first three Jacobite bids for power, between 1708 and 1719, failed.

Charlie's Year

By the time of the last Jacobite rebellion in 1745, the cause was already lost. London had grown too powerful: Lowland Scotland, despite occasional mob riots in Edinburgh against Government action, was beginning to get used to being part of Britain. Forts were built to keep the Highlanders in check, the English General Wade built the region's first good roads and bridges, and a Highland regiment, the Black Watch, was incorporated into the British army to police the glens. It was against this background that clan chiefs met the young Prince Charles Edward Stewart—"Bonnie Prince Charlie"—when he landed in the Outer Hebrides from France with just seven followers, determined to fight for what he saw as his birthright. Go home, they told him. I have come home, he replied.

It was not really true. This elegant young man in a powdered wig, grandson of James II, had been raised in France—hence his other nickname, the Young Chevalier. He spoke poor English and no Gaelic;

he had not visited Scotland before. All he had in his favor was his burning ambition to win the throne of Britain (he would not have been interested in fighting just for Scotland) and a forlorn hope that the French might help him.

Somehow, despite knowing the futility of the struggle, many chiefs rallied to Charles's standard, raised at Glenfinnan in August 1745. They called what followed *Bliadna Thearlaich*, Charlie's Year. Perhaps they knew the old way of life of the clans was doomed, and preferred to go out in a blaze of glory. Soon the Prince was marching on Edinburgh with a Highland army three thousand strong. They captured the capital without bloodshed. The citizens seemed to receive the Prince and the proclamation of the new regime enthusiastically.

Charles's hopes soared. His morale, and that of his soldiers, increased still further when they routed the English army in Scotland at

Prince Charles enters Edinburgh in 1745 at the head of an army of Highlanders. His challenge to the British government was to prove short-lived. British Museum

Government redcoats and Highlanders clash at Culloden in 1746—the last battle to be fought on Scottish, and indeed British, soil.   Her Majesty Queen Elizabeth

Prestonpans. The English, with their disciplined ranks of red-coated musketmen, their cavalry and their powerful artillery, broke before the impact of the legendary Highland charge. The Highlanders charged on foot, a small, round, studded shield called a *targe* in one hand, a heavy broadsword called a *claymore* in the other.

After dallying in Edinburgh, Charles set out for London in October with some eight thousand foot soldiers and three hundred cavalry. Although there was panic in southern England, and King George II made plans to evacuate his palace, the Jacobites never really had much chance. Their only hope of beating the thirty thousand regular English troops massing against them was if the French intervened. The French did not. In December, at Derby, Charles and his army—already much weakened through desertions by Highlanders who never dreamed they

· 158 ·

would be away from home for so long—turned back for Scotland.

The final showdown came just a few months later, on Culloden Moor, east of Inverness. Charles had found much of Lowland Scotland closed against him on his return, and by the time he confronted a large, well-trained, well-supplied government force led by the Duke of Cumberland, the Jacobite army numbered scarcely five thousand men. They were hungry, poorly equipped and, on the morning of the battle, exhausted from a failed night attack on government positions. After a ferocious pounding from Cumberland's artillery, the Highlanders charged across open ground. The redcoats stood firm and cut swathes through them with fusillades of musket fire. When it came to hand-to-hand fighting, the Highlanders discovered that the English soldiers had been trained to thrust their bayonets not at the man facing them but at the man on their right, who would be vulnerable with his sword arm raised. The clans were slaughtered. Charles escaped and roamed the Highlands as a fugitive, with a gigantic price on his head. No Gael betrayed him. One day a French warship sailed up a sea loch and took him away, to die in lonely and embittered exile.

Retribution and Clearance

The vengeance wrought on the Highlands by the government, which meant Lowland Scots as much as English, was harsh. The wounded clansmen on the field of Culloden were killed where they lay. Escaped rebels were hunted down: Many were captured and executed or sent overseas as convicts. The wearing of tartan and traditional Highland costumes was banned. No Highlander was permitted to carry arms. Even the bagpipes were outlawed. On a more subtle level, the government drew the Highland chiefs into London's high-society world of landowning nobles and senior military officers, dissolving the family ties between them and their clans. Fighting clansmen were recruited in huge numbers to serve in the British army, where they served with great courage and heavy losses all over the world.

The final blow to the old Highlands came when the new-style chiefs, now mere landowners looking to make as much money as possible from their estates, discovered the potential of the Cheviot sheep. This hardy breed, rich in wool and fat with mutton, could happily graze the roughest mountainside and moorland—creating far more profits than did the tenants scratching a living from their crofting lifestyle. In the interest, they claimed, of improvement and progress, landowners began a sustained, ruthless campaign to clear tenants off their land to make way for sheep, the "four-footed clansman." Families were evicted at a few hours' notice and their homes burned. This brutality, known as the Highland Clearances, continued until the mid-nineteenth century. The Highlanders' exodus was hastened after the great potato famine of 1846 (the potato had by then become their staple diet). Those evicted found jobs in fishing ports, moved to the expanding cities, or emigrated by the thousands to Canada, the United States and Australia. Many would find better lives there, but the manner of their parting from the land they loved was cruel, as this eyewitness account from Skye shows:

There were old men and women, too feeble to walk, who were placed in carts; the younger members of the community on foot were carrying their bundles of clothes and household effects, while the children, with looks of alarm, walked alongside. . . . When they set forth once more, a cry of grief went up to heaven, the long plaintive wail . . . was resumed, and after the last of the emigrants had disappeared behind the hill, the sound seemed to re-echo through the whole wide valley of the Strath in one prolonged note of desolation. The people were on their way to be shipped to Canada.

Lochaber No More, *painted in 1883 by J. W. Nicol. Members of a small Highland community, forcibly evicted by their landlords to make way for sheep, take a last look at their homeland before sailing for a new life overseas.* Robert Fleming Holdings

CHAPTER XIV

The Spirit
of Invention

Reading, Writing and Revolutions

Within a few years of the last Jacobite uprising, gradual changes in society, hardly noticeable before, were gathering pace to create an explosive transformation in the nature and status of Scotland. By the end of the eighteenth century, the dramatic effects of three revolutions—agricultural, industrial and mental—were plain for all to see. But these revolutions would have ripped apart and rewoven the fabric of Scotland less quickly had it not been for the country's acceptance at a much earlier date of the virtue of universal education.

In 1560, John Knox urged that every Scottish parish and burgh should have its own school. The dream was not realized straight away. But because post-Reformation Scotland both feared and respected the Kirk, and since the Kirk favored schools for all, education came to be seen as a good and desirable thing. By 1696, when the Scottish Parliament ordered a school for every parish, many had one already, as did many burghs. The expansion continued until at least the mid-eighteenth century, by which time virtually everyone in the rural Lowlands—that is to say, most of the population in Scotland—could read and write. In this, Scotland was far ahead of most of the rest of the world. And it meant the seeds of new ideas then blowing through the world would find fertile ground in which to grow.

Revolution: Agriculture

Scotland at the time of the Union had, in common with most of Europe, a very inefficient style of agriculture that had remained unchanged for centuries and laid the nation open to famines equal to those suffered by developing countries today. The land was divided into narrow strips on which the same crops were grown year in, year out, until the soil was exhausted. Much land was wasted.

But change was afoot. Scottish landowners were bringing ideas home with them from visits to Holland and England, ideas they quickly put into practice on their own estates. The blanket of long, thin strips was turned into a neat checkered pattern of square fields, enclosed by hedges and dykes (walls). New crops like potatoes and rutabagas were introduced. Fields were chemically fertilized for the first time, and crops were "rotated"—a crop that took goodness out of the soil would be followed by one that put nutrients back in. Marshes were drained to create new farmland. The monotony of the landscape was relieved with tree plantations. Given their own pastures and proper food in winter, cattle grew fat. Faster, cheaper horse-drawn plows replaced the old kind, pulled by gangs of oxen. By 1820, the Scots were producing at least twice as much food as they had in 1770.

Although the ideas of the "improvers" met fierce resistance from many tenants, all of whom faced a complete change of lifestyle, the transition went forward with little of the anguish and cruelty of the Highland Clearances. Many of those who had worked the land switched to jobs in the new textile industries that were springing up. Those who remained became sharply divided. Where before, the laird's subtenants had lived close to peasants, both farming the same strips of land and grazing livestock on common turf, there was now a farming class and a laboring class. A farmer would control a large acreage of adjoining, enclosed fields, and would pay local workers with no land of their own to tend beasts, sow, harvest and carry out farm chores.

Revolution: Industry

The changes that affected Scottish farming were dramatic. But the country's switch from a rural society unable to manufacture even its own sewing needles to a powerful industrial economy, which by the 1900's supplied the world with a quarter of all its shipping, was little short of miraculous.

Before the middle of the eighteenth century, power-driven machines and factories were as unknown to Scotland as to the rest of the world. Anything manmade was made by hand or by using the simplest of hand-driven apparatus. But new English inventions were about to change this, and when they came to Scotland, they found a society ready to receive them. It was a stable society, with the last echoes of Jacobite gunfire dying away. It was, as shown above, a relatively well-educated society, receptive to new ideas and trained by the stern sermons of the Kirk to believe in the virtue of hard work. It was a society able to trade freely with the increasing number of British colonies overseas. Never so rigidly divided between upper and lower classes as other European nations, it was a society where a bright youngster from any but the poorest background could get ahead. And it was a society that at long last had cash available for investment, as merchants such as the Glas-

James Watt in his workshop. Watt's radical redesign of the steam engine gave the Industrial Revolution the power to change the face of the world.

gow tobacco lords made huge fortunes. Much of the tobacco from the Virginia plantations was handled by Scottish traders.

The first impact of the industrial revolution was on the field of textiles. A series of English inventions made it possible to use water power—of which Scotland had an ample supply—to drive machinery that could spin hundreds of threads of cotton simultaneously. The first Scottish cotton mill appeared in Rothesay in 1778, and through the 1780's many more were built, mainly south of Glasgow. Innovation followed innovation. Steam engines replaced water power, meaning mills could move to towns and cities. Ways were devised to weave as well as to spin cotton on an industrial scale. As the nineteenth century progressed, cheap wool, linen and jute fabric also began to pour from Scottish factories.

As steam became more important, more fuel was needed. Mines

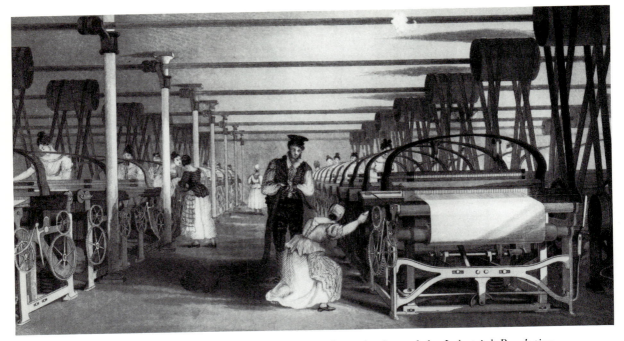

A typical textile factory shop floor from the early days of the Industrial Revolution.
British Museum

became deeper and more numerous, and the first canals—including one
that linked the Forth and the Clyde—were cut to carry coal. Demand
for coal came, too, from the iron industry. Scotland's first major industrial complex had been the Carron ironworks near Falkirk, founded in
1759. By the 1830's, iron was being produced in Central Belt furnaces
from local coal and local ore.

At about this time, the second phase of the industrial revolution
began in earnest, as the scale and profits of the textile factories began
to be eclipsed by those of the steel and engineering works. This was the
time of Queen Victoria's reign—the Victorian Age, when the British
Empire was at its most powerful, and Scottish engineers established a
legendary reputation. From the 1840's on, railways began to snake
across the country, linking the great cities and the smallest market
towns. Among the feats of the railway builders was the monumental
bridge across the Forth, the immense red girders of which still carry

express trains from Edinburgh to the northeast, a testimony to the can-do spirit of an age when anything seemed possible. Shipyards and shipping lines sprang up, particularly around the Clyde. The shipbuilders started by building sailing vessels: They ended up with the *Queen Mary*, the world's mightiest ocean liner. By the late nineteenth century, it seemed the whole Central Belt heaved with smokestack energy, churning out battleships and locomotives and marine engines for all the world, breathing coal dust and iron ore, the sky red at night with the glow of crucibles of molten steel. The country's technological dominance was to prove short-lived, and had always been costly in terms of human suffering; but to have created so much in so little time was a great achievement.

Adam Smith: First Apostle of Capitalism

Merchants in Europe and in the European colonies overseas had been grappling with the increasingly complex patterns of international trade for many years when, in the mid-eighteenth century, a young academic named Adam Smith sat down at his desk in Kirkcaldy to write *An Inquiry into the Nature and Causes of the Wealth of Nations.* His work, when published, reached far beyond the day-to-day mechanics of taxes and who paid how much for what. For the first time, theories were offered about the links between wages, prices, rents and profits, revealing how together they underpinned man's culture and history. Although his arguments in favor of unbridled free enterprise, and against state interference in trade, rightly mark him as a major influence on defenders of big business, his focus on history's economic basis was influential across the whole political spectrum. Karl Marx, whose work *Das Kapital* provided the theoretical base for communism, respected and drew from Smith's ideas.

Revolution: Thought

The eighteenth century was a time of great change not only in material things but in the way Europeans thought about the world. The agricultural improvers and the textile barons in Scotland carried out their schemes in the name of progress, but the idea of the human race progressing and bringing nature under its control was relatively new. In Britain, in France, in colonial America, it was an age that saw scientists and thinkers looking at the world and striving from careful observation and logical thought to draw up the first laws governing physical phenomena and human behavior. When people applied the same process of rational thought to society as a whole, a few of them decided society was not following the proper laws; and the first steps were taken on the road to the American and French Revolutions.

For such a small country, Scotland's contribution to the eighteenth-century Enlightenment, as it came to be known, was extraordinary. For a few brief decades a set of brilliant and original minds made the country a byword for genius throughout Europe and beyond. Foremost among the Scottish thinkers was the Edinburgh philosopher David Hume (1711–1776), whose book *A Treatise on Human Nature* cut through all past certainties about the way the world was experienced. After Hume, no scientist or politician could ever again answer the question "Why?" with a glib "Because that's how it's always been."

Alongside Hume as he laid the foundations of modern philosophy was Adam Smith (1723–1790), a professor at Glasgow University, who virtually created the science of economics single-handed. From the work of Adam Ferguson (1723–1816) and John Millar (1735–1801), sociology was born; and William Robertson (1721–1793) was among the few great men in Europe toiling to write history as we know it today, based on intensive research from original source material. In 1791, Robertson

Scotland: Cradle of Ideas

The Scots' talent for innovation has not been confined to the period of the Enlightenment and the Industrial Revolution. Their ideas, often brought to a successful conclusion when the Scots concerned worked outside their homeland, are woven deeply into the fabric of our technology-dominated century.

James Clerk Maxwell (1831–1879) was acknowledged by Albert Einstein as the greatest physicist since Isaac Newton. Born in Edinburgh, his education and his working life were divided between Scotland and England. His theories about electricity and magnetism showed the way to those who would, much later, invent radio and other forms of electromagnetic-wave broadcasts.

Sir James Young Simpson (1811–1870) developed chloroform as the world's first practical anaesthetic while working as a medical professor in Edinburgh.

Alexander Graham Bell (1847–1922), born in Edinburgh, emigrated as a young man to the United States, where he invented the telephone.

John Logie Baird (1888–1946), of Helensburgh, developed the world's first working TV system in 1929. It was a commercial failure, however, as it relied too heavily on cumbersome means to transmit and receive a picture.

Sir Alexander Fleming (1881–1955) was born in Ayrshire but studied in England, and achieved his greatest triumph there when he discovered the antibiotic drug penicillin. In 1944 he was awarded the Nobel Prize for medicine.

New Images of Scotland

At the very point in history when large parts of Europe were at last becoming safe, comfortable, tame places for the well-off middle classes to live, these same people developed a craving for "Romantic" literature. This consisted of books and poetry that described wild, remote scenery or featured characters who seemed in touch with a more primitive, uncomplicated way of life. Sir Walter Scott's historical novels, set against a background of real events and real places that were glorified and crowded together like scenes in an epic movie, were lapped up by this audience. As for Robert Burns—writing poems and lyrics of simple brilliance in his native Scots—he was hailed as a natural genius, a living part of the very landscapes Scott portrayed. However warped this view of the writers, it changed the attitudes of England and Europe toward Scotland. When Scott's first novel, *Waverley*, was published, the Scottish tourist industry was virtually invented overnight. Scotland was no longer seen as a dull, wet country inhabited by lazy, ignorant savages, but as a patchwork of romantic landscapes, ancient heroes and folksy, down-to-earth people. So it has been, in

published his *History of America*, and his ideas about scholarship—he was Principal of Edinburgh University—formed the basis of the modern American educational system.

Scots were equally active in the field of science. Eighteenth-century scientists were like benign conquistadors, setting out on voyages into the unknown with the most primitive of equipment, conscious only that there was a universe to discover and rich prizes within it. In the vanguard were James Hutton (1726–1797), who paved the way for all

the eyes of much of the world, ever since. Here is an extract from a poem by Scott in which the modern reader can clearly visualize the writer's eyes misting with rosy sentiment as he recalls the sources of his inspiration:

> Methought that still with tramp and clang
> The gateway's broken arches rang;
> Methought grim features, seamed with scars,
> Glared through the window's rusty bars,
> And ever, by the winter's hearth,
> Old tales I heard of woe or mirth,
> Of lover's slights, of ladies' charms,
> Of witches' spells, of warriors' arms:
> Of patriot battles won of old
> By Wallace wight and Bruce the bold;
> Of later fields of feud and flight,
> When pouring from the Highland height,
> The Scottish clans, in headlong sway,
> Had swept the scarlet ranks away.

(*Wight* means brave. The "scarlet ranks" are British redcoats.)

subsequent geologists; Joseph Black (1728–1799), who discovered carbon dioxide, then switched from chemistry to physics to work out the theory of latent heat; and Daniel Rutherford (1749–1819), who discovered nitrogen.

There was another set of more practical thinkers in Scotland, who had more direct influence on the development of the world and on the lives of ordinary people: the inventors. Actually, "designers" would be a better word, for most so-called inventors, like America's Thomas Alva

Edison, were for the most part brilliant improvers of existing ideas.

The classic example is that of James Watt (1736–1819), the Greenock engineer who turned the steam engine from a wheezing, feeble pump into a machine of enormous power that could power trains, ships and factories—and even today drives the turbines that give us most of our electricity. But there were many others. John Macadam (1756–1836), from Maybole near Ayr, pioneered modern road surfaces ("tar Macadam" became tarmac). His roads were improved on by Thomas Telford (1757–1834), the son of an Eskdale shepherd, a great civil engineer who built more than seven hundred miles of sound Highland roads, more than a thousand Scottish bridges and the Caledonian Canal along the Great Glen between the North Sea's Moray Firth and the Atlantic Firth of Lorne. Scotland's shipbuilding and marine engineering industries owed much to William Symington (1763–1831) and Patrick Miller (1731–1815), who launched the world's first practical steamship, the *Charlotte Dundas*, on the Forth-Clyde Canal in 1802.

In the arts, notably in literature, architecture and painting, a similar flowering happened in the late eighteenth and early nineteenth centuries. In the poetry of Robert Burns (1759–1796) and the novels of Sir Walter Scott (1771–1832), Scotland found voices that would carry something of the country onto the bookshelves and into the imaginations of half the world. The popularity of their work was not entirely due to the genius of these two writers: They were lucky in that they were active at the very time when a newly literate audience craved the type of work they produced. Europe's view of Scotland was transformed as a result.

Progress and the People

The Scots Who Stayed

The industrial and agricultural revolutions made Scotland a far richer country, and one in which scarcely anyone had to starve. A handful of Scots entrepreneurs became enormously wealthy. Thousands of small farmers became prosperous, and were able to afford fine furnishings, expensive clothes and an unaccustomed variety of food and drink. In the expanding towns and cities, a growing middle class—lawyers, doctors, Kirk ministers, shopkeepers, engineers, civil servants, accountants, architects—enjoyed similar comforts.

But this prosperity was achieved at the cost of exhausting labor and suffering on the part of the majority of the Scottish people. Exploited through low wages and long hours, crammed into overcrowded tenements, buffeted by slumps in whatever industry they worked in and victims still of poor diet and disease, the lot of many ordinary urban workers was grim.

Scotland's population soared. From about 1.25 million in 1750, it reached over 2.5 million in less than a century. More and more people moved from the countryside to the large cities and new industrial towns that sprang up around rural mills and mines. They came from the more efficient Lowland farms (where fewer hands were needed), from the Highlands, and from Ireland. Glasgow, once known as the fairest Scottish city, grew huge and ugly. In 1755, it had just over 30,000 inhabitants. By 1821, the number had risen to 147,000. By the 1900's, a fifth of all Scots lived there—and by this time the country held about 4.5 million people. This increase was reflected on a smaller scale in every town, particularly those like Airdrie, near Glasgow, which had scarcely existed before the Industrial Revolution.

Women and children were exploited shamelessly by employers. In the textile mills of the late eighteenth and early nineteenth centuries, children as young as nine years old worked twelve to fourteen hours a day, six days a week, with two days' holiday a year. Mill owners found that women and children could be paid lower wages, and could be coerced more easily than men into accepting the mechanical, repetitive factory toil, so alien to a people used to the clockless rhythms of farming life. Conditions in the coal mines, particularly those in Fife and Lothian, were worse still. Wives and daughters were expected to haul their husbands' and fathers' coal up to the surface from where they had hewn it. In the eastern pits in the early decades of the nineteenth century, girls as young as six would spend a fourteen-hour day carrying loads as heavy as a hundred pounds (45 kilograms) from coalface to above ground. Such atrocities were not halted until the government passed the Mines Act of 1842, one of a series of measures designed to protect women and children from the harshest labor. Most effective of these was the Education Act of 1872, which made school compulsory for all aged between five and thirteen.

City Chambers, George Square, Glasgow. One of the magnificent Victorian buildings erected by a proud and confident Scottish business community in the nineteenth century.
Author

Housing for the urban Scottish working class in the nineteenth and early twentieth centuries was often appalling. Property speculators grew wealthy by cramming ramshackle tenements together and crowding huge families into tiny spaces. An 1861 census recorded two thirds of the population living in houses or apartments of either one or two rooms. By 1911, half the country's people remained in the same predicament. In these unsanitary conditions, with drinking water as often as not seriously polluted and smoke and fumes belching from factories, diseases like typhus, cholera and tuberculosis wreaked dreadful havoc.

As the era of the urban population explosion began, it found civic leaders completely unprepared for—and in many cases uninterested in—the health and housing crisis that made so many Scots' lives a misery. But wealthier townsfolk, motivated by conscience as much as unease at what they saw as the political powder keg of discontented workers, gradually organized proper town councils to tackle the worst problems. Glasgow took the lead in this. Some schemes were inspirational, like that which in the 1850's replaced the city's vile water supply with pure water from the hills. Others, like the slum clearance programs, left troublesome legacies that linger to this day. But right up until World War I, Glasgow's council continued with great success to extend its responsibilities into every area of life, providing an example to all Scotland of how a city authority could create useful services for its citizens that would otherwise not have existed. One observer writing in 1903 said a Glaswegian could

. . . live in a municipal house; he may walk along the municipal street, or ride on the municipal tramcar and watch the municipal dust cart collecting the refuse which is to be used to fertilise the municipal farm. Then he may turn into the municipal market, buy a steak from an animal killed in the municipal slaughterhouse, and cook it by the municipal gas stove. For his recreation he can choose amongst municipal libraries, municipal art galleries and municipal music in municipal parks. . . .

The Scots Who Left

By the middle of the eighteenth century, Ulster was beginning to be rivaled as a destination for emigrant Scots by the expansion of British colonies overseas. The British Empire was born in the eighteenth century in North America and India as a series of trading outposts and as an extension of European wars. The habit of taking over other people's countries and firmly forcing on them the virtues—as the settlers saw

· 176 ·

it—of British civilization grew into an addiction for conquest that the loss of the United States only fueled. By its peak in 1897, the Empire covered 11 million square miles. The British flag, the "Union Jack," waved over Canada, Australia, New Zealand, India, Hong Kong, Singapore, huge tracts of Africa from Cairo to Cape Town and countless other states in every continent and ocean. Then, within a single lifetime, it waned rapidly through two world wars, independence movements among overseas colonies and the rise of the superpowers. Now it is history.

Through every phase of the Empire's existence, Scots took advantage of the opportunity to break out of their crowded, impoverished country to what must have seemed fantastic opportunities in the new colonies. There were great farms and plantations to work, minerals to be mined, native peoples to be suppressed and administered, mammoth civil engineering projects to be undertaken. If it occurred to any of the Scottish emigrants that there was a parallel between their feeling of superiority over the natives of the colonies and the historic arrogance of the English toward them, they did not show it.

The exodus seldom slackened. Scotland's population would have become much larger in the twentieth century if half the people in the natural population increase had not left between 1900 and 1920. Between 1920 and 1930, the population actually fell.

Although the poorer emigrants were often forced to leave under bitter circumstances, and although the Atlantic voyages took a horrifying toll in lives from disease on board overcrowded ships, many if not most of the Scottish families that settled in Canada, Australia and New Zealand did indeed find greater prosperity overseas. English-speaking Canada, in particular, was born on the crest of a Scottish wave. By no means all Scots went to British colonies, of course, and the next most favored destination outside the Empire was the United States. Two Scots, John Witherspoon and James Wilson, signed the Declaration of Independence. After the 1850's, the United States began taking in more Scottish immigrants than Canada. Between 1921 and 1930, for instance, almost 160,000 Scots settled there.

From among its huddled masses Scotland sent forth numerous individuals who grew famous through special deeds and events in the annals of Victorian Britain. There was the missionary-explorer David Livingstone, for example, a passionate evangelist and campaigner against the Arab slave trade in Africa. He marched on arduous journeys of exploration throughout the length and breadth of that continent, unmapped and hostile to foreigners, dying in the jungle in 1866, at the age of fifty-two, before he could discover the source of the mighty River Nile. There was Dunfermline-born Andrew Carnegie, who, aged thirteen, emigrated to Pittsburgh on borrowed money, built up a massive industrial empire of iron, coal, steel and railroads, sold the lot and gave away $350 million to good causes around the world. There was Lachlan Macquarie, who turned Australia's New South Wales area from a penal colony to a working, civilized state by giving convicts proper status within the community.

The Fight for Democracy

Political activity did not stop dead in Scotland with the Union of Parliaments in 1707. It took more than two centuries before anything like democracy as we understand it today was won. But that struggle, though it had its uniquely Scottish aspects, has to be seen against a broader background of campaigns across the whole of Britain for reform of corrupt London government.

Many issues wove themselves into post-Union Scottish politics. There was a great split in the Kirk, which saw ministers divide into an establishment church and an evangelical church, the Free Church of Scotland. There was the antialcohol Temperance Movement. But the two intertwined causes that created Scotland's modern political colors were electoral reform and, in various guises, socialism.

Although in 1707 the King or Queen of Britain and the British Parliament's unelected upper chamber, the House of Lords, retained considerable influence on the government, this influence was on the wane. It was the elected lower chamber, the House of Commons, that would come to wield most power. As the eighteenth century progressed, clear political parties formed: Whichever party had the most members in the Commons was the party that ruled the country. If no party had an overall majority, parties would form alliances that became known as "coalition governments." The eighteenth century also saw the emergence of the role of Prime Minister, initially the royal representative in the Commons, eventually the leader of the dominant party and the leader of the nation.

It was clear at the start of the Union that Scottish Members of Parliament (MPs) would always be outnumbered by English, Welsh and Irish members. Still, they were there to put forth the Scottish point of view, and had the potential to decide on key issues affecting Scotland.

But only a few thousand Scots, mainly merchants and landowners, had the vote. The rural areas and burghs that sent MPs to Parliament did not reflect the population patterns of the country, resulting in huge distortions as cities and towns expanded. Corruption and bribery of voters was rife because there were so few. The Scottish contingent in Parliament were puppets in the hands of powerful party managers, who were able to dish out important government offices as favors to those who played it their way.

Reform did not begin seriously until the nineteenth century, and proceeded with agonizing slowness. Deprived of democratic representation and faced with terrible economic injustices, many Scots took to militant action both to change the electoral system and to right more immediate wrongs.

Major turmoil first broke the surface in the backwash of the American and French revolutions. The latter's message of "Liberty, Equality, Fraternity" struck a powerful chord in the minds of many Scottish working people when the revolution erupted in 1787. Robert Burns, then a customs officer, even sent three cannons, captured from a smuggler, to France's revolutionary army. An organization called the Scottish Friends of the People was formed, campaigning for votes for all and new parliamentary elections every year. The government reacted ruthlessly, putting leading spokesmen on trial and sentencing them to long terms of hard labor in the Australian penal colony (a punishment called "transportation").

Equally harsh treatment was meted out to the handloom weavers, a group of literate, practical, independent-minded workers hard hit by competition from new power-driven weaving machines. In 1787, when a group of Glaswegian weavers, in a bid for higher pay, attacked the property of manufacturers, three weavers were shot dead by troops. Throughout the early years of the nineteenth century, weavers across the country pressed Parliament for a legal minimum wage; but Parliament did not act, and the weavers formed a union. In 1812, they went on strike. After a couple of months, the leaders of the Glaswegian union were arrested, tried on a dubious charge and imprisoned. The strike collapsed.

By this time revolutionary France had turned into an aggressive empire, bent, it seemed, on conquering all Europe, including Britain. Scotland was drawn closer to England in the face of a common threat, and many Scottish soldiers fought as part of British forces overseas. But with the defeat of the French in 1815 came an economic slump, and calls for reform were renewed.

The first hesitant steps toward changing the unfair electoral system came in 1832, with the Reform Act. It increased the number of Scots allowed to vote by about sixty thousand, and redrew the electoral boundaries so the big towns and cities were represented more fairly. But the majority of Scotsmen, like the majority of Englishmen, still had no say in the government of the country. And women had no vote at all. Parliament remained deaf to pleas for change from mass movements such as the Chartists, who presented them with petitions that bore more than a million signatures demanding voting rights for all males, and other electoral and economic reforms.

Only toward the end of the nineteenth century did the legislature bestir itself to further reforms. Yet the Third Reform Act, passed in 1884, still left four tenths of Scotsmen and all Scotswomen without a vote.

The two main parties in Parliament at this time were the Tories (also known subsequently as the Conservatives) and the Liberals. Generally, the Tories stood for the traditional idea of a natural social pyramid with wealthy landowners at the top and poor, simple workers at the bottom. The Liberals, the dominant party in Scotland until 1922, consisted of a mixture of more democratically minded wealthy people and radical reformers of every social background. It was the Liberals who eased through nineteenth-century reform measures after the failure of Chartism.

As the twentieth century approached, however, the Liberal Party began to be overstretched as the conflicting ideas held by its members and supporters covered increasingly extreme right-wing and left-wing positions. In parts of England, right-wing Liberals deserted to the Conservatives. In Scotland, some saw the best hope for the future in socialism, a cause that embraced not only electoral reform but also a string of pledges to combat the evil side effects of industrial progress— poor housing, poor health, low wages, long hours, unemployment, and a general lack of welfare provision for children, the sick and the elderly. The result was the formation of the Labour Party.

The Scottish Labour Party was founded in Glasgow in 1888. It was not a socialist party as continental European socialists would have understood it; although it drew its support almost exclusively from blue-collar workers, its guiding principles stemmed as deeply from the humanitarian Christianity of the New Testament, with its message of equality and pacifism, as from any Communist manifesto.

Labour's hour did not come immediately. The Liberals held on, introducing radical measures such as a comprehensive social security system. In 1914, the First World War broke out. Britain and France squared up against Germany and Austria-Hungary. To the dismay of pacifist Labour founding fathers like James Keir Hardie, Scots flocked to join the British army. Their losses, added to civilian casualties, amounted to almost 150,000 dead. In the last year of the war, 1918, the Liberal-led coalition government finally gave the vote to a significant proportion of the people: all men over the age of twenty-one, and all women over thirty. In an election held the same year, the Liberal Party's policy of keeping socialism at bay by introducing its own social reforms seemed to be paying off in Scotland, which elected just six Labour MPs.

But already there were signs of militant socialist activity, particularly in Glasgow, parts of which had earned the nickname "Red Clydeside." There were strikes and protests by the Clyde Workers' Committee, a group of radical socialist trade unionists in Glaswegian engineering factories. These culminated in a riot in 1919 in the city's George Square after police charged striking workers. Some believe to this day a workers' revolution similar to that which had ushered in the Soviet state in Russia two years earlier was just barely prevented. The government was worried enough to send tanks and troops with machine guns to guard key points in the city. The government also made martyrs of leading left-wingers, such as the eloquent revolutionary socialist John MacLean, by frequently imprisoning them.

A more successful protest than that of the Clyde Workers' Committee came from the wives of Glasgow servicemen and munitions workers,

George Square, Glasgow, 1919: With the Russian Revolution, which gave birth to the Communist Soviet Union, only two years old, the Government feared a similar upheaval on "Red Clydeside." When mass protests like this one by striking workers were organized, London sent tanks and troops to the city. Locally garrisoned Scottish units of the British army were confined to barracks, and strike leaders were arrested. After the police broke up the demonstrations, government fears of insurrection faded. Glasgow Herald

who refused to pay steep rent increases imposed on them by wartime profiteers. Faced with the threat of workers themselves putting down their tools in support, the government gave in and froze rents by law.

The increased support in Scotland for the socialism of the Labour Party was made clear in the election of 1922, when the country elected twenty-nine Labour MPs, nineteen of them from the west of Scotland.

This support was reflected across Britain as a whole, and the eclipse of the Liberals was soon complete. But the Scots Labourites' uncompromising pledges to champion the underdogs of their country were softened by their stay in London. Their rough edges smoothed by the clubbish atmosphere of the House of Commons, where MPs of all parties relaxed together as friends outside the debating chamber, their egos massaged and ideals tempered by their first taste of power (five Scots sat in the Cabinet of Britain's first Labour government, in 1924), they became increasingly moderate in outlook.

Labour has secured more votes than any other party in Scotland in all but two of the nineteen general elections since 1922. The exceptions were in the 1930s, the grim Depression years when unemployment reached undreamed-of levels and Scotland's traditional heavy industries went into irreversible decline. The radical and the desperate embarked on protests outside official politics—for example, the general strike of 1926 and the hunger marches of the 1930's. But neither these nor the formation of the Scottish National Party in 1928 attracted enough support to reject the London government, during this period a Conservative-dominated coalition.

The Second World War, which broke out in 1939, casting the horror of Nazi Germany against Britain and its allies, served to put the seal on Scotland's acceptance of a powerful London-based government—providing that the government, which would preferably be Labour, was committed to a well-planned economy with adequate welfare provision for the needy and proper awareness of the special needs of Scotland.

Scotland sent its usual contingent of servicemen to fight the war. Although German bombers did not hit Scotland as severely as England, they wreaked dreadful havoc, in Clydebank particularly, where at least 1,000 Scots died. Armaments poured from Scottish shipyards and factories, and a determined war against German submarines was waged from

Panel 6 of Scots artist Ken Currie's epic mural depicting the struggles of Scottish working people through the ages. Painted in 1987, this panel is called "Fight or Starve . . . Wandering Through the Thirties." On the left, protest marchers of the Depression years: on the right, men and women work to defeat Nazi Germany, symbolized by the swastika on the cobbles. People's Palace Museum, Glasgow

Scottish ports and airfields. The Germans and Japanese were beaten.

In 1944, the last great army to muster in Scotland came together in Edinburgh. Hundreds of thousands of men from all the Allied nations, with their tanks and trucks and artillery, were gathered within the city. In fact, the army did not exist. It was a decoy, assembled only on paper in order to deceive the Nazis as to where the real invasion of Europe would take place. It was also an appropriate symbol for the capital of a country that, for better or for worse, was firmly wedded to England, Wales and Northern Ireland in one United Kingdom. Though Scotland remained a real nation, the idea that its people would ever again take up arms against the rule of London was inconceivable.

Art and Culture

Scottish Literature

Out of all the arts, Scots have excelled in literature—novels and poetry especially. For such a small country, Scotland has produced a remarkable number of writers who have loomed large on the world stage. Why should this be so? The early introduction of education for all no doubt played a part. Another factor could have been Scotland's poverty. Opera, orchestral music and painting all required support from rich patrons, in short supply in Scotland. Writing required only spare time, paper and ink—not readily available to many Scottish working people until recently, true, but if they could be found, writers could at least create finished works without further help.

The Death of Scots

The golden age of literature in the medieval Scots language came in the late fifteenth and early sixteenth centuries. It centered on the courts of James IV and James V. For the first time there was wealth and leisure enough to support a number of good writers, who showed that the Scots language shared by the King and his people was not only well formed and unique, but also capable of expressing great beauty and profound thought.

By the time one of the best of these writers, the poet William Dunbar (approximately 1460–1520) came to pen his *Lament for the Makaris*—about the poets who had died before him—a literary tradition had been established. The Wars of Independence had inspired two long poems that mixed historical facts with an effort to create and immortalize larger-than-life Scots heroes. These were *The Brus* (Bruce) by John Barbour, archdeacon of Aberdeen, published in about 1375; and *The Act and Deeds of Sir William Wallace* by "Blind Harry," written shortly before James IV ascended the throne.

The great poet Robert Henryson was just ending his career as Dunbar was beginning his. Greatly influenced by the English poet Chaucer, Henryson translated the fables of Aesop, an ancient Greek author, into clear, rhythmic Scots. In an age when the works of ancient Greeks and Romans were seen as the most important pieces of literature, writers who could translate them into Scots gave their language extra status as a result. Another important Scots poet, Gavin Douglas, followed Henryson's example when, just two months before the Battle of Flodden, he completed a translation of the most famous Roman poem, Virgil's *Aeneid*. This was before any English poet had successfully taken on such a task. Douglas's work is a triumph, not just as a straight translation but as a transfer of the spirit of the tale from its Mediterranean setting to a new North Atlantic background. Here is a taste, a description of the ferryman Charon, whose role in Greek mythology was to take the dead across the River Styx:

> *Thir ryveris and thir watyris kepit war*
> *By ane Charon, a grisly ferryar,*
> *Terribil of schap and sluggart of array,*
> *Apon his chin feil cannos harys gray,*
> *Lyart feltrit tatis; with burnand eyn red,*
> *Lyk twa fyre blesys fixit in his hed;*
> *Hys smottrit habyt, owr his schulderis lydder,*
> *Hang pevagely knyt with a knot togiddir.*

> *[These rivers and these waters were kept*
> *By one Charon, a grisly ferryman*
> *Terrible in shape and slovenly clad,*
> *Upon his chin many gray hairs,*
> *Withered, matted tufts; with burning red eyes,*
> *Like two firebrands fixed in his head;*
> *His stained costume, slouching over his shoulder,*
> *Hung peevishly knit with a knot together.]*

It was the Protestant Reformation that spelled the beginning of the end for Scots as a literary language, and what that did not change, the Union of the Crowns did, forty-three years later.

The Kirk disapproved of drama and music. The collapse of Catholicism also meant court poets could no longer gain a living from holding posts within the church. The atmosphere in Scotland became hostile to nonreligious writers. Then, when James VI and his court traveled south to settle permanently in London, the seedlings of Scots literature were torn up by the roots to wither in an alien climate.

It was James VI who put the final nail in the coffin of Scots as a clearly defined literary language when he sponsored the preparation of an "authorized" English edition of the Bible. Here was the most important book of all, available to the masses for the first time, the only book many people would ever have in their homes. Had an edition been prepared especially for Scotland, in Scots, young writers would have grown up with its phrases ringing in their ears, and the language could have been preserved. As it was, the King James Bible appeared only in English—an English, as it turned out, of tremendous power that made the book one of the most brilliant translations ever to be published. Faced with this, the cause of Scots was doomed. How ironic, then, that the next and brightest-ever Scottish star to shine did use a descendant of Scots in his writing. But he was alone in his time, and has been alone since: There was only one Robert Burns.

Robert Burns

Robert Burns (1759–1796) is a unique phenomenon in world literature, a poet and lyricist whose work, despite being written in an obscure dialect, appealed and continues to appeal to people at every level of society, in every country of the world. He was born in Alloway, near Ayr, the son of a poor farmer. As an adult he worked as a customs officer. Although he became famous throughout the British Isles, he never managed to clear his family's debts before he died.

Burns was not a callous womanizer, as he is sometimes portrayed, but a man who loved women. He was not a drunkard, but a man who loved drink and good company. He was not a calculating observer of society, but a man who loved life. His humanity, his passion for equality among all people, his awareness of his very human vices, break down any barriers that his use of Galloway Scots might have put between him and his audience. And his genius framed his feelings in verse of perfect tempo and clarity. Small wonder he is toasted and recited at annual Burns Suppers from Montreal to Moscow. Small wonder his version of the old Scottish song "Auld Lang Syne" is sung in every conceivable

Robert Burns, painted in 1786 by Peter Taylor.   Scottish National Portrait Gallery

tongue, including Japanese.

Many of his best-known poems, such as "A Man's a Man for A' That," express his belief that no one should think himself or herself better than anyone else—in social status, or in terms of being good or bad:

> *Ye see yon birkie, ca'd a lord,*
> *Wha struts, and stares, and a' that;*
> *Though hundreds worship at his word,*
> *He's but a coof for a' that:*
> *For a' that, and a' that,*
> *His ribband, star, and a' that,*
> *The man of independent mind,*
> *He looks and laughs at a' that.*

[*birkie*—fellow; *ca'd*—called; *coof*—fool; *ribband*—ribbon; *a'*—all]

Usually his verse is inhabited by the ordinary folk of southwest Scotland, the farmers and ministers and bartenders he knew so well. Sometimes other beings are present, as in the supernatural tale of poor drunk Tam O'Shanter, who stumbled across a band of dancing devils late at night:

> *There sat auld Nick, in shape o'beast*
> *A towzie tyke, black, grim, and large,*
> *To gie them music was his charge:*
> *He screw'd his pipes and gart them skirl,*
> *Till roof and rafters a' did dirl.*
> *Coffins stood round, like open presses,*
> *That shaw'd the dead in their last dresses;*
> *And by some devilish cantraip slight*
> *Each in its cauld hand held a light.*

[*towzie tyke*—shaggy dog; *gie*—give; *gart*—made; *dirl*—rattle, *cantraip slight*—weird trick]

Scottish Novels: Truth Through Fantasy

The subject matter of *Tam O'Shanter* is nothing unusual for a Scots writer. One of the hallmarks of Scottish literature has been the use of fantasy, horror and the supernatural not only to tell a story but to pass on a message about the nature of mankind. Scottish novelists in particular have wrung and twisted the fabric of the national realities they portray to create half-comic, half-grotesque alternative images. It is significant that literary treatment of three of the world's classic horror themes have originated in Scotland: the artificial creation of life by Dr. Frankenstein (an invention of Mary Shelley, inspired by her Dundee childhood); the undead feeding on the living, as in Count Dracula (the work of Bram Stoker, inspired by sojourns at a castle near Arbroath); and the scientific transformation of human into superhuman, first portrayed in 1896 in *The Strange Case of Dr. Jekyll and Mr. Hyde* (by Edinburgh's Robert Louis Stevenson, equally well-known for *Treasure Island*).

The greatest Scottish novel to fall into this category is *The Private Memoirs and Confessions of a Justified Sinner,* by the Borders writer James Hogg. First published in 1824, it is a devastating satire on the perils of extreme Calvinism—on people who believe they are born destined to reach Heaven, no matter what atrocious sins they commit. The central character, Robert Wringhim, is one such man, goaded into committing ever more terrible crimes by a shadowy "friend" who turns out to be the Devil. The book succeeds in many ways: as black comedy, as the study of a tormented soul, even as a guide to the gloomier side of the Scots character.

Two modern Scottish writers, Alasdair Gray and Ian Banks, have taken up the idea of truth through fantasy in their novels. Gray's *Lanark*, an immense book in every sense of the word, is partly a realistic story, loosely based on the author's early life, about a confused, frustrated artist growing up in the west of Scotland through the thirties, forties and fifties. To this Gray welds a parallel tale about a journey through a strange, dark land that emerges as a nightmarish caricature of Strathclyde. The novel caused a sensation when it first appeared in 1981. Impossible to digest at a single reading, it shows a breadth of imagination and delight in the limitless possibilities of prose all too rare in modern fiction. One of the characters is the author himself, who has his own thoughts on what he is doing:

He began speaking in a shrill whisper which swelled to a bellow: "*I am not writing* science fiction! Science-fiction stories have no people in them, and all my characters are real, real, real people! I may astound my public by a dazzling deployment of dramatic metaphors designed to compress and accelerate the action, but that is not science, it is magic! Magic!"

Why should Scots writers be so ready to tread into the realms of fantasy and the supernatural? Perhaps they feel hemmed in. Scotland is a small country, and there are not many Scots. Lacking the huge land areas and populations of the Soviet Union or the United States, they may feel the need to set their stories against a big background—such as the infinite spaces of their imagination.

Kailyard to Renaissance

Stevenson apart, the late nineteenth and early twentieth centuries were famine years for Scottish literature. Scots writers expended what energies they had on smug, sentimental moral tales of virtue rewarded and hardships overcome. These were the years of "kailyard" literature, when writers looked no further than their own backyards for themes and inspiration.

Overseas, however, new ideas were stirring. The First World War, the Russian Revolution and the advent of cinema gave impetus to a global wave of "modernism," of artists determined to seek radically new directions in their work. This movement had its effects on Scotland, effects by tradition grandly described as the Scottish Renaissance. Certainly, compared with the literary slumber into which the country had fallen, there was an awakening—one that would fuel Scotland's writers right up to the present day. But the talent of the "Renaissance" was concentrated within very few individuals.

Foremost among these was Hugh MacDiarmid (1892–1978), a strong-willed poet of great passion and power. Born in the old county of Dumfriesshire, he had a number of different jobs, but spent much of his life in poverty. At one time in the 1930's he was a member of both the Scottish Communist Party and the Scottish Nationalist Party, which he helped found in 1928. (Both parties expelled him when they found out!)

His ambition was to revitalize Scottish literature by combining the use of Scots, virtually abandoned since Burns's time, with some of the ideas of the Modernists. This meant attacking the narrow-minded, old-fashioned, provincial thinking of fellow Scots and injecting his verse with a good dose of twentieth-century politics and philosophy. His best work is in his own style of Scots—a mixture of the dialect he knew and long-forgotten words found only in dictionaries. In his long poem *A Drunk Man Looks at a Thistle*, he roams wide and free over subjects from love and alcohol to Scotland's place in the world. Yet he was capable of expressing himself in the simplest and shortest of poems, such as "The Bonnie Broukit Bairn":

> *Mars is braw in crammasy,*
> *Venus in a green silk goun,*
> *The auld mune shak's her gowden feathers,*
> *Their starry talk's a wheen o'blethers,*
> *Nane for thee a thochtie sparin',*

Earth, thou bonnie broukit bairn!

—But greet, an' in your tears you'll droun
The haill clanjamfrie!

[*braw*—good; *crammasy*—crimson; *goun*—gown; *mune*—moon; *gowden*—golden; *wheen o'blethers*—piece of nonsense; *nane*—no one; *thochtie*—slight thought; *broukit*—neglected; *bairn*—child; *greet*—weep; *droun*—drown; *the haill clanjamfrie*—the whole shebang]

The other major figure of the Scots Renaissance was Lewis Grassic Gibbon, best known for *A Scots Quair*, a set of three novels dealing with life in the Mearns (a rural area west of Stonehaven). *Sunset Song*, *Cloud Howe* and *Grey Granite* describe the life of a farmer's daughter from childhood to old age. In the process they chart the great shift of the Scots from the countryside to the towns and cities. Gibbon tells his story in a straightforward, fluid style, sprinkling his mainly English text with enough dialect words to give it a northeastern flavor. His starkly realistic portrayal of the harshness of Scottish rural life at the end of the last century contrasts sharply with the idealistic vision conjured up by those who were actually writing at the time.

Writing Today and the Language Problem

Scots writers have always faced a dilemma over which language to use. Just how do you define Scottish literature? Most eighteenth- and nineteenth-century Scottish novelists used English no different from that used by English writers such as Jonathan Swift or Charles Dickens, though they gave their work Scottish settings. At the same time Burns would have gotten nowhere if he had confined his genius to the strait-

jacket of his English verse (which was mediocre). Back in the sixteenth century, George Buchanan was famous throughout Europe for his poetry and drama, hailed as the greatest of the age. Who remembers him now? Practically nobody, for he wrote in Latin. Yet he, too, was Scottish. Are the modern Gaelic poets the only real Scottish writers, or does the solution lie in carefully representing on the printed page the authentic speech patterns of twentieth-century Scots? The argument stands today at a healthy simmering point.

While his work is firmly rooted in Scotland, for instance, Alasdair Gray writes in what is more or less English English, happy for his work to be in a world language that hundreds of millions can readily understand. Poet Tom Leonard, on the other hand, writes his verse in such a way that even non-Scots reading the syllables carefully out loud would find themselves speaking Glaswegian. James Kelman, yet another west-coast author and Scotland's best living writer of realistic fiction, concerns himself with capturing the rhythms of Glasgow speech, leaving the accent up to the reader. As things stand today, all modern Scottish writers find the solutions that please them most.

Stage and Screen

Muffled after 1560 in the disapproving blanket of the Reformation, Scotland has yet to produce a playwright of world stature, a Shakespeare or a Molière or an Ibsen. The nearest to these in terms of fame was James (eventually Sir James) Barrie, born in Kirriemuir in 1860. He later settled in London. His numerous plays have not stood the test of time—with the single, immortal exception of the classic *Peter Pan*.

The poet Hugh MacDiarmid.   Scotsman Publications Ltd.

But the twentieth century, and the postwar period in particular, has seen a growth in Scottish drama. Innovative theater companies have been formed, producing new Scottish plays, reviving forgotten Scottish classics and introducing Scottish audiences to the work of exciting foreign dramatists. Foremost among these has been the touring 7:84 Company, which took the radical political message of its first production, *The Cheviot, the Stag and the Black, Black Oil*, to little-visited sites in the Highlands in 1973; and the Glasgow-based Citizens Theatre, which has since its foundation in the 1960's achieved a worldwide reputation for adventurous productions.

Every year, Scotland hosts the world's largest arts festival, the Edinburgh Festival, first held in 1946. Its size does not stem from the official festival, a rich but conventional selection of music, opera, art and ballet; it is accounted for by the Festival Fringe, a vast catalog of stage productions performed by companies from all over the world. For several weeks, every theater, church hall and gym in the city plays host to one of several hundred plays, stand-up comics, mime shows and musicals. Groups travel from as far away as Japan and Australia to take part. In the 1980's, Glasgow has gradually built up its own annual arts festival, the Mayfest, to rival the capital's.

Scotland accounts for about one tenth of the United Kingdom's population, but produces a far smaller proportion of its television and movies. British TV has four main channels (although, at the time of writing, cable and satellite TV are set to take off). The British Broadcasting Corporation, or BBC, funded by a levy of about $100 per year per TV-owning household, has two channels, as does the independent, commercially funded network. All have their main production bases in the south of England, and most Scottish television consists of a mixture of English and American programs. But the Glasgow studios of BBC Scotland and the independent station STV do manage to produce more than local news magazines, turning out documentaries, single plays, and series like the award-winning *Tutti Frutti*, a black comedy by John Byrne about the round-Scotland tour of an aging rock-and-roll band, The Majestics.

Architecture

However poor Scotland's early inhabitants, the need for defense against the weather and against human enemies ensured that architecture would be the first art to flourish.

Stone has always been the prime Scottish building material, whether the granite of the northeast or the rich red sandstone used to face whole streets of Glasgow tenements. The bricks of England and the wood of Scandinavia seem alien even now. Stone was quarried thousands of years ago to make the bottle-shaped brochs that dot the landscape of the northern and western isles. Until recently, the traditional way of dividing up Scottish farmland was the "drystane dyke"—a wall of unmortared stone.

What has been created from this abundant natural resource? Certainly the Scots have in the past made buildings that are masterpieces of design and beautiful to look at. But is there anything that is uniquely Scottish? Looking at the fruits of the great days of medieval religious building, fine as they are, the answer must be no. The monasteries and abbeys built between the twelfth and fourteenth centuries follow European patterns, with the church and living and sleeping quarters grouped around a central "cloister," a roofed-over walkway supported by pillars. The story is the same with Scotland's thirteen medieval cathedrals. The best of them, like those at Glasgow, Dunblane and Elgin, are eloquent testimony to the skill and dedication of master craftsmen who would labor over them for all their working lives without the aid of written plans or modern machinery. But it would be hard to pinpoint anything about them that was not an imitation of work done elsewhere in Europe.

Domestic Castles and Fortified Homes

Turning to castles, the picture is different. Scotland has a vast number of castles and fortified houses, and military architecture influenced the design of quite humble Scottish buildings right up until our own century.

In the beginning, Scottish castles were simply walls surrounding clusters of ordinary buildings—stables, a feasting hall, an armory. Over the years the walls became strong, well-finished stone structures studded with towers and a massive gatehouse. Eventually the rooms built over the gate became the living quarters of the lord who owned the castle and his household.

So far there was little difference between Scottish castles and those in the rest of Europe, except that the Scottish ones tended to be smaller and less comfortable. But during the sixteenth and early seventeenth centuries a distinctively Scottish style did emerge. "Scottish Baronial," as it has come to be called, developed because wealthy Scots landowners wanted a more luxurious lifestyle. When the Reformation released to them much of the wealth of the old Catholic Church, they had money to build more comfortable houses, better finished inside and more decorative outside. But at the same time Scotland remained a dangerous, lawless country, where restless nobles and plundering Highlanders—not to mention the English—could still run riot through the

Sixteenth-century Claypotts Castle, in Broughty Ferry, Dundee. Its stout stone walls and small windows are designed primarily for defense, but comfortable living quarters on the upper floor show a shift from military to domestic architecture was under way.   Author

countryside. As a compromise, "tower houses" were built.

Scottish baronial tower houses have the tiny windows, narrow stair-cases, battlements and turrets one would associate with a medieval fortress. But inside their upper floors, as at Claypotts Castle in Dundee, owners would strive to create the same comfort and atmosphere of fine living enjoyed by the wealthy citizens of more law-abiding countries like England and France. A version of the same style appeared at the same time in the burghs.

Victorian architects were fond of borrowing elements of Scottish Baronial design. In Marchmont, for example, an attractive nineteenth-century tenement district in Edinburgh (now monopolized by students from Edinburgh University), tenements on the corner of each block boast slim pepperpot turrets, harking back to the days of the tower house.

Designs for Living: Edinburgh's New Town

Scotland has produced a number of individuals whose architectural and design ideas have spread out to inspire the wider world. It was appropriate that the general explosion of talent centered on eighteenth-century Edinburgh should produce one such character—James Craig, whose 1767 design for a new area of housing north of the city's castle was one of Europe's earliest and best examples of town planning. The smelly, overcrowded maze of narrow wynds and closes making up the Old Town of Edinburgh represented a great incentive to create an airy, spacious, straightforward scheme. Craig's broad New Town streets were laid out in an elegant grid pattern, punctuated by squares and crescents and public gardens. The four- and five-story terraced homes built then stand unchanged today: stern, strong ranks of gray stone descending down the slope from the foot of Castle Rock to the district of Leith beside the

Forth, long since split up into apartments, and a little pollution blackened, but still revealing a whitish-gold luster when the sun strikes them.

Designs for Living: Robert Adam

Craig died in 1795, before his great plan was completed. Others had already been at work, extending his original ideas. Among them was Robert Adam (1728–1792), the most celebrated architect Scotland ever produced. Adam had the perfect background for his chosen career in an era when rich landowners were finally abandoning castle-style homes in favor of spacious mansions, set in carefully designed ornamental parks. While the eighteenth century saw many of the scientific ideas of the ancient Greeks and Romans discredited, their architecture—called "classical"—became hugely popular. Adam's father, also an architect, had worked under the Scottish pioneer of the classical style, William Bruce. Adam followed in his father's footsteps. In 1754, he set off on a trip to Europe. He stayed in Italy for several years, soaking up the lessons of the ruins left by the Romans. He believed he saw how the Romans had really worked, how they had not been fettered by artificial rules as the early eighteenth-century classical architects imagined.

When he returned to Britain, to settle finally in London, he quickly achieved worldwide fame as much for the overall interior design of his creations as for the way the buildings looked on the outside. His style of decoration, easy to duplicate, appeared on everything from crockery to furniture: It was a free, creative borrowing of the countless emblems and sculptures he had seen as ornaments on the ancient ruins of southern Europe. People liked it because it added a fashionable classical facade to anything it adorned, without being too heavy, formal and expensive. The State House in Boston, Massachusetts, was just one of the buildings outside the British Isles created as an imitation of the

Adam style. Adam himself, with his brother, a partner, put it this way:

We flatter ourselves we have been able to seize, with some degree of success, the beautiful spirit of antiquity, and to transfuse it, with novelty and variety, through all our numerous works.

Designs for Living:
Charles Rennie Mackintosh

Like Adam, Charles Rennie Mackintosh (1868–1928) was eager to design not just the structure of a building, but all that went inside it. Mackintosh was a unique figure in Scottish architecture, a brilliant master of color, shape and texture in materials as diverse as stone and mother-of-pearl. He wanted to lead British design away from the cluttered, gloomy interiors of the Victorian era, to a style that did not depend on endless copying of the art of previous centuries. But though he attracted praise and admiration at exhibitions in Vienna, Turin and Moscow, he was little admired in his own country. In 1914, with his career waning, he was forced to leave his native Glasgow for England, where he spent the rest of his life. Only recently has his genius been recognized.

Mackintosh got little chance to exercise his talent on major public buildings or large country houses, as his less adventurous colleagues did. His biggest commission was the Glasgow School of Art, but his best work can be seen in his interior design. He would take an ordinary room and transform it into the most human kind of artistic creation—one that could actually be lived in. In the study at his Glasgow home, for instance, he flooded the room with natural light by enlarging windows, then made the room still lighter with all-white walls and floor. Against this background he placed just three pieces of furniture, each of his own

Eighteenth-century Culzean Castle, on the southwest coast. Designed by Scots architect Robert Adam, its turrets and battlements are in fact ornaments on what is essentially a luxurious country mansion. Part of it was given by Scotland to General (later President) Eisenhower, in gratitude for his successful command of Allied forces in the Second World War. Author

design. Their style is bold and straightforward, a set of black and white squares and rectangles and single curves, set off with subtle decorative motifs of ivory, leaded glass and mother-of-pearl. Every last detail in the room—the cubic brass lampshade pierced with red glass teardrops, even the cushion on the chair—is designed to harmonize with the overall concept.

Mackintosh's vision could have shown Scottish designers a middle way between the much-admired elegance of Japanese homes and traditional European styles, but Scotland was not prepared to learn.

Music: The Songs

Every nation sings its joys and troubles, and every nation sings of love and grieving with its own voice. Scotland is no exception. From the earliest days of the Gaelic bards to the modern folk band's guitar, fiddle and accordion, Scots have been raising their voices in song.

The two main strands of Scottish song are the Gaelic and the Lowland Scots, of which the Gaelic is the older. Gaelic verse was traditionally composed to be sung rather than spoken. It was not written down until very recently, but was memorized and passed from generation to generation through the ages.

The oldest Gaelic songs still to be heard in the Hebrides and in the northwest survive, little changed, from medieval times—perhaps even from the time the Gaels crossed into Scotland from Ireland around 500 A.D. Sung in a steady, chanting style, they recount the legends of Irish warrior heroes, battles of Gaels against Norsemen, magic rowan trees and monster sea hags. A later tradition of Gaelic songs comes from the compositions of the great clan bards of the seventeenth century. Every clan had its bard, to sing the praises of the Chief, to commemorate great battles and to remember the old songs. The best professional bards were expected to be able to memorize 350 different poems and tales.

A very different style of Gaelic song survived in everyday life at least until the 1960's: the work songs, sung to accompany tasks like rowing, milking, reaping, grinding corn. Most numerous were the "waulking songs," sung by the women of a Gaelic community as they sat round a narrow table, cleaning and thickening a band of newly woven cloth with their hands to make it ready for use. The thump as they banged the cloth on the table in unison gave the songs a steady, powerful beat.

The work songs no longer have a major place in Highlanders' day-to-day lives, as twentieth-century technology replaces oars with outboard motors and removes the need for traditional ways of making textiles like the famous Harris tweed. But all kinds of Gaelic music is kept alive by schools, by local choirs and by professional musicians. The biggest event of the Gaelic cultural calendar is the National Mod, held in a different town each year, where musicians from all over the world compete for prizes. Entrants travel not just from Britain but from countries like Canada and the United States, where communities of Scots descent make up important alternative guardians of the Gaelic heritage.

In contrast to the well-remembered songs of the Gaels, many of the songs and ballads of Lowland Scotland are lost to us. But by the early seventeenth century, English-speaking Scots were beginning to write them down. In 1718, wigmaker-turned-publisher Allan Ramsay brought out the first book of Scottish song lyrics; and in 1725, singer William Thomas produced his *Orpheus Caledonius*, with both words and music. The greatest collector and preserver of Scots songs, however, was Robert Burns himself. Working in the late eighteenth century, he recorded vanishing lyrics and filled in gaps in songs of which sometimes only the title remained. He set existing songs to Gaelic tunes, or wrote his own words to go with the music.

A deluge of Scots songbooks poured from the presses in the wake of Burns's and Ramsay's work. (Novelists James Hogg and Walter Scott were also avid song collectors.) The way these pioneers operated means the rich legacy of printed Scottish song texts and music handed down to us is a curiously hybrid collection, though reflecting all in its own way its country of origin. The original singers of the stirring "Bonnie Dundee," for instance, might not have recognized Walter Scott's anglicized version, despite the odd Scots word thrown in:

> *To the Lords of Convention 'twas Claverhouse spoke,*
> *Ere the King's crown go down there are crowns to be broke:*
> *So each cavalier who loves honour and me,*
> *Let him follow the bonnets of Bonnie Dundee.*

The words of the melancholy "Over the Sea to Skye" ("Skye Boat Song"), about Prince Charles Stewart's flight from Culloden, also sound more English than Scottish—yet it is sung to a tune based on Gaelic rowing songs:

Speed, bonnie boat, like a bird on the wing
Over the sea to Skye.
Carrying the lad that was born to be king
Over the sea to Skye.

On the other hand, the Borders ballad "Jock o' the Side," one of the innumerable musical tales of the cattle-thieving feuds between English and Scottish nobles, sounds little changed from the way it would have been sung by the person who wrote it down:

Now Liddesdale has ridden a raid
Wi' my fa ding diddle lallow dow diddle;
But I wat they had better hae staid at hame;
For Michael o' Winfield he is dead,
And Jock o' the side is prisoner ta'en
Wi' my fa-ding did-dle lal-low dow-di-dle.

In the end, it was Burns who fused new and old together most successfully in his reworkings of traditional songs. He did not greatly anglicize what words remained of the originals, and he filled the gaps with lyrics that were fresh, free of clichés and true to his own genuine Scottish voice.

Scots have never stopped making up new songs to fit new circumstances, or adapting their own new words to old tunes. The trials of life in a Victorian city brought songs like this one, sung with a slow, sad keening that gives its simple words a sense of the desperate weariness that inspired it:

O dear me
The mill runs fast

The poor wee shifters
Cannae get a rest
Shifting bobbins, coorse and fine,
They fairly mak ye work
For your ten and nine.

[*coorse*—coarse; *ten and nine*—ten shillings and nine pence, the singer's wage in old British money]

Scottish farming life since the eighteenth century has been the subject of the "bothy ballads," a jaunty set of sentimental tales, extended jokes and songs about hiring and firing, all seen from the point of view of the "bothy," the hut where farm laborers lived. New bothy ballads continued to be composed in the twentieth century, with every new facet of agricultural technology being worked in—such as the replacement of horses by tractors:

O I'm just a fairm servant and a tractorman by trade
I drive a dual-power Major, the best tractor ever made
She can cultivate and harra, aye, an' pull a muckle ploo
And the wheel grip o' yon tractor has nae equal up tae noo.

[*harra*—harrow; *muckle ploo*—big plow; *tae noo*—to now]

Scottish emigrants took their gift of song across the Atlantic to America, where it was thrown into the melting pot along with English, Irish, Spanish and African folk music to create the popular sounds of the twentieth century. There are particularly strong links between Scottish folk music and American country-and-western and hillbilly music—both of which are very popular in Scotland.

When rock-and-roll began in the United States in the 1950's, there were immediate British attempts to imitate it. It did not take Britain long to catch up, and the U.K. has teetered between the first and second slot in the world rock and pop rankings ever since. Britain's music industry was very much London-based, however, until in the late 1970's a group of rebellious new English bands inspired young musicians outside the capital to start performing and recording songs without waiting for a big London record company to sign them up first. Ever since then a steady stream of Scottish groups and individual performers have made their mark on the charts on both sides of the Atlantic: Simple Minds, Annie Lennox of the Eurhythmics, Big Country, Aztec Camera.

The world of English-language rock music is more or less uniform as far as accent is concerned. Most singers from England adopt an American-style accent for their songs. The same has usually been true of Scottish singers, with only the odd vowel or rolled "r" betraying their origins. But at least one 1980's duo, the Proclaimers, has given its music an uncompromisingly Scottish flavor in terms of accent and subject matter. Intriguingly, this proved no obstacle when in 1987 they went to number three in the influential British Top 40 with their single "Letter from America," comparing the deserted homelands of emigrant Highlanders with the derelict factories of modern Scotland:

> *When you go, will you send back*
> *A letter from America?*
> *Take a look down the rail track*
> *From Miami to Canada*
> *Broke off from my work the other day*
> *I spent the evening thinking about*
> *All the blood that flowed away*
> *Across the ocean to the second chance*
> *I wonder how it got on when it reached the promised land?*

Music: The Bagpipes

The history of Scotland's national instrument goes back thousands of years, to the day people discovered how to make a musical note by

A patriotic piper on the streets of Edinburgh.   Scotsman Publications Ltd.

blowing air through a reed fixed to the end of a hollow pipe. Add fingerholes, as the inhabitants of the ancient city of Ur did in about 3,000 B.C., and you have the first reed instrument. How and when the bag came in, and how the bagpipes reached Scotland, remain a mystery. Some say the Romans introduced them, others that the Caledonians invented them independently, others that they were imported from the Mediterranean long before the Romans arrived.

In medieval Europe, most countries had a type of bagpipe. They were part of medieval dance bands, playing at festivals, market days and royal entertainments. Scotland was always one of the keenest patrons of bagpipe music. Until the early nineteenth century many Lowland towns employed a town piper, an honored citizen with a special uniform whose duty it was to pipe the town awake in the morning and pipe it to sleep at night.

But it was in the Highlands that the bagpipe found a lasting foothold. There, in the sixteenth century, just as the rest of Europe was abandoning the instrument as a quaint relic of more primitive times, the Mac-Crimmons—hereditary pipers to Clan MacLeod—were creating a new style of pipe music. This was the *piobaireachd*, or "pibroch" in English spelling. Instead of a simple tune, the pibroch would open with a theme, which would then be developed over a sequence of variations into a haunting musical scheme of orchestral depth.

The pibroch lifted the bagpipe into another class of instrument, and helped it survive and flourish to the present day in Scotland, when in most other nations it has become an obscure, occasional guest at folk-band performances. The great Highland bagpipe, which led the clans to battle at Culloden, lived through subsequent banning as a weapon of war to be incorporated into the Scottish regiments of the British army. Although present-day civilian pipers play in competitions, at New Year, at weddings and just for fun, the military and police marching pipe-and-drum bands are the performers modern Scots are most likely to hear.

In its present-day form, the Scottish Highland bagpipe consists of six distinct parts: the bag (made of cloth-covered sheepskin), the chanter, the blow-pipe and three drones. The bag is tucked under the piper's arm and blown into to inflate it. The pressure of the elbow on the bag forces air through the chanter, which has finger holes to play different notes, and through a double reed like that of an oboe to make the actual sound. Air is also forced through the drones lying across the piper's shoulder, each of which has a single reed inside, sounding a constant note to harmonize with the melody played on the chanter. The advantage of the bagpipe is that the music need not be interrupted by the piper taking breath. Pipers can blow into the bag when they like, as long as it is full enough to keep a steady stream of air flowing through the chanter.

The pibroch is rarely heard these days, with pipers preferring to air more accessible tunes in public. But the instrument's piercing, haunting tone, emerging from the sound of the drones like a needle sewing silver thread through coarse linen, never fails to affect listeners, whatever tune is played. Whether that means a nostalgic tear in a Scottish emigrant's eyes, hearing the pipes played by foreign bandsmen in some former British colony like Canada or Pakistan, or a grimace and fingers in the ears, it is a music that, once heard, is not forgotten. There are now hundreds of pipe bands around the world, including the United States, which hosts several piping summer schools each year. By no means all pipers claim Scottish ancestry.

Scotland's Place Today

Scotland in Britain

How firmly is Scotland wedded to the other countries that make up the United Kingdom of Great Britain—Northern Ireland, Wales and the dominant England? In some respects they seem as closely linked as branches of the same tree. There is no fence, no customs barrier, no police checkpoint at the roads that cross the Scottish-English border. Scots and English are governed by the same London-based British Parliament, to which both send representatives according to their respective sizes. They carry the same British passport and the same British driver's license, pay the same British taxes and are defended by the same British armed forces.

At the same time, as already shown, Scots do regard themselves as different. They are separated from England by clear-cut differences: by their different laws, schools, church, accent, customs, history. The question remains of modern Scotland: Is it likely in the future to become bound more closely to England, or less?

In the decades following the defeat of Prince Charles and the Highland army at Culloden, right up until the end of the First World War, Scottish politics closely followed the politics of Britain as a whole. It had the same political parties as England. Indeed, considering the nationalist fervor that swept mainland Europe in the nineteenth century, giving people as diverse as the Norwegians and Hungarians a yearning for independent republics, it is remarkable how seldom the ordinary Scots' struggle for a say in the affairs of their country expressed itself in a desire to be detached from England again. Easy communications with their English-speaking fellow campaigners across the border, the continuous safety valve of emigration for frustrated Scots and a desire to remain at the heart of an apparently supreme economic and political world power, the British Empire, all contributed to the lack of political nationalism in Scotland.

During the same period, however, Scots began to develop a kind of split personality—one that most retain to this day. A lack of interest in taking positive action toward independence went hand in hand with a growing obsession with a watered-down version of Scotland's past culture and history. Encouraged by the pressure of enthusiastic tourists from all over the world, drawn to the country by the rosy picture painted in Sir Walter Scott's novels, the Scots began to bask in the glories of their dead heroes. Traditional Scottish songs were subtly rewritten to be acceptable to the English and presented as genuine. Music-hall entertainers, such as Harry Lauder, dressed up in ludicrous versions of Highland dress and performed on the English stage as caricature Scots. Many Scots were hugely flattered when Queen Victoria fell in love with the Highlands and took to spending holidays there.

This brittle picture, with Scotland wallowing in a lost independence it had no interest in regaining, began to splinter with the terrible impact of the First World War. More than eighty thousand young Scotsmen went to their deaths in the muddy trenches of France and Belgium. For some Scots, as for many other Europeans, a romantic, sentimental picture of the world was no longer possible.

Two political currents flowed from the period between the two world wars: Scottish socialism and Scottish nationalism. As already seen, the socialist Labour Party has dominated Scottish politics since the 1920's, with the right-wing Conservative Party its main rival. Neither movement had much to do with independence.

The Scottish National Party (SNP), founded in 1928, was the first organized group to campaign for an independent Scotland. For years it remained on the fringes of politics. But the movement began to gather strength after the Second World War. Scots' dissatisfaction with their country's slow rate of recovery from old economic wounds, and a general feeling that the London government did not understand Scotland's unique nature, led in 1967 to SNP success. A nationalist candidate overturned a huge Labour majority in Hamilton to become the first SNP Member of Parliament. In 1974, the SNP won seven parliamentary seats; in a fresh election the same year they won eleven, more than one seventh of the total number of Scottish MP's. The Labour government of the day acted by drawing up plans for Scotland to have its own assembly with limited powers to pass laws. Opposition from many MP's inside and outside Scotland was fierce, and the government gave the Scots a chance to vote for or against their plan—"Devolution," as it was called. The Scottish electorate voted in favor by a narrow margin. But the government had declared beforehand that at least 40 percent of the entire electorate had to say yes before Devolution would go ahead. The actual figure was 32.5 percent. At the next election, the fateful 1979

The Scottish National Party rallies supporters at the site of the Battle of Bannockburn, on the battle's 674th anniversary. In the background is a statue of Robert Bruce, who led Scotland to victory in the Wars of Independence.   Scotsman Publications Ltd.

contest that saw the Conservative administration of Margaret Thatcher sweep to power, the discredited SNP lost all but two of their seats.

The Devolution schemes of the 1970's would never have given the Scots much more than a forum in which to air their grievances. The proposed assembly would have had less power than a state legislature in the United States: It would not have been able to levy taxes, for instance. It would have been a start, perhaps, and would have helped

Scotland preserve its identity and culture. But it would have gone nowhere toward realizing one of the key aims of the SNP's campaign: unlocking the treasure chest of North Sea oil revenue—wealth that under present arrangements, flows directly to the British government for distribution around the whole U.K.

Are the Scots still interested in any kind of political independence? The answer is almost certainly yes. But how? In a way, the Scots have voted for independence at every election since the mid-1970's, even though they have not given the SNP overwhelming support. By giving Labour a huge majority of Scottish MP's when England was giving the majority of its votes to the Conservatives, the Scots continued to state their political difference. The trouble is that because so much of Labour's support comes from Scotland, Labour is now the party least likely ever to let the country go its own way. Three conditions are necessary for any independence movement to succeed in the future: an alliance between the SNP and a new Scottish Labour Party, separate from English Labour; a severe economic slump to make enough Scots question the existing political order; and an articulate, intelligent, charismatic leader or leaders. None of these conditions exist at the time of writing: All are perfectly possible in the future.

Suppose, then, that Scotland was able to extract itself completely from the rest of the United Kingdom. How would it fare? Economically, it would have the major advantage of secure supplies of energy. Although reserves of North Sea oil are starting to run down, Scotland could adopt the Norwegian strategy of cutting production down to a low, constant, long-lasting level, instead of going all out for maximum production as at present. Scotland also has major reserves of coal and peat, and gets a small but significant proportion of its power from hydroelectric installations. Experiments in generating electricity with large windmills have begun on the gale-swept islands of the north and west, and ways may one day be found to exploit the waves that pound the country's long coastline.

Nuclear power already supplies a large proportion of the country's energy needs, and few Scots realize how much that proportion is set to increase. No less than six tenths of Scotland's electricity will eventually come from nuclear stations—a higher proportion than in any other country in the world except France. This situation has come about not because the Scots are particularly pronuclear (if anything, they lean toward an antinuclear stance), but because decisions on the siting of nuclear plants are made in London, and the impetus is strong to site them in remote coastal areas. To many English political-decision makers, Scotland as a whole can be considered such an area. But these decisions have left Scotland with a legacy of surplus electricity that gives it hefty economic muscle.

The Scottish economy is also beginning to haul itself out of the rut it was stuck in after its old Victorian heavy industries went into terminal decline. Nowadays it is much more broadly based. Traditional industries such as whisky making and engineering are bolstered by a huge, well-organized tourist industry and by the host of foreign electronics companies that have made their European base in the Silicon Glen between Edinburgh and Glasgow. A government-sponsored organization, the Scottish Development Agency (SDA), has made great strides in bringing new employment to Scotland. It makes loans to promising Scottish companies, builds factories and warehouses and encourages overseas firms to set up in the country. The SDA's five overseas offices—in Brussels, Belgium, and in the American cities of Chicago, Houston, San Francisco and Stamford—are perhaps the nearest thing to embassies that today's nonindependent Scotland has.

But there are weaknesses. The country is overreliant on foreign investment. When a trade slump strikes, companies pull the plug on

Protestors against homelessness outside the Scottish Office in Edinburgh, through which the London government rules Scotland.   Scotsman Publications Ltd.

their overseas operations first, and that leaves Scotland vulnerable. Although Scottish scientists and engineers remain at the forefront of some areas of research—artificial intelligence, for example, and fiber optics—all too often their ideas end up being used in the designs of overseas companies. Some would argue that the Scots themselves are to blame for this, claiming that they have lost the spirit of initiative that fueled the industrial revolution of the eighteenth century. Others would say that if Scotland had its own government, then talent, bright ideas and cash for investment would not flow from the country so rapidly.

Another weakness lies in the sheer scale of poverty, unemployment and bad housing in some parts of Scotland. There would be little point in breaking away from the rest of Britain if these shadows could not be lifted from the country. But would Scots have the courage to face up to decades of possible hardship while their nation's resources were used to defeat them?

Scotland in Europe

The relationship between Scotland and the rest of Britain is being increasingly affected by Britain's links with Europe. The key link is the European Community, or EC. Britain is one of the EC's twelve member states, the others being France, Germany, Italy, Spain, Greece, Portugal, Denmark, the Irish Republic, Holland, Belgium and Luxembourg.

The EC is also known in Britain as the Common Market, a name that sums up the main reason for its foundation. Its aim is to create within member countries, whose combined populations reach well over 300 million, a gigantic trading zone without tariff barriers or any kind of restrictions on the movement of citizens. Much has been done toward this end already. A Glaswegian bricklayer is free to work on a building site in Germany without a work permit; a teacher from Paris can settle in Edinburgh without filling out any forms. By 1992, common regulations on goods and services will enable Scottish businesses from banks to breweries to operate in Madrid or Athens or Copenhagen without the complexities of setting up separate overseas operations. A common passport for all EC citizens and standard EC driver's licenses are already being issued.

The EC has problems that go beyond the obvious one of the language barriers between member nations. To many Scots, the EC still seems to mean no more than a bureaucracy that hands over massive subsidies to farmers. The surpluses that have resulted, the "wine lakes" and "butter mountains," have become the first Europe-wide standing joke. Scots wonder, too, at the European elections held every few years, in which they elect members of the European Parliament, an assembly that meets in Strasbourg, France, and in Brussels, Belgium, and has no powers whatsoever.

Living in the EC's extreme northwestern corner, few Scots yet share the vision of some idealistic Europeans, who seek nothing less than a full-blown United States of Europe, with a common currency and a common foreign policy. But the railway tunnel now being built under the sea between Britain and France, the Channel Tunnel, may subtly alter Scottish thinking on this. Who knows what effect it will have on the psychology of all the inhabitants of mainland Britain—for thousands of years used to living on an island—when a fixed link is finally completed to the rest of Europe, and hence to Asia and Africa?

More importantly, the federation that could now be emerging from the clouds of national prejudice that divide the states of Europe might usher in a new era for Scotland. Instead of striving to catch up with the rest of the continent by winning independence for itself, Scotland might see the rest of Europe trying to imitate its own unique constitutional position. It is not impossible to imagine a future Europe composed of a host of semiindependent states, whose relationship with a European government would mimic Scotland's relationship with London: states with their own laws, customs and languages, but without separate control of foreign policy, defense, and major economic issues.

Scotland in NATO

Britain was one of the founders of the North Atlantic Treaty Organization (NATO) after the Second World War. Formed to counter what was seen as a threat from the Soviet Union, NATO welds the armed forces of countries such as the United States, Canada, West Germany and Italy

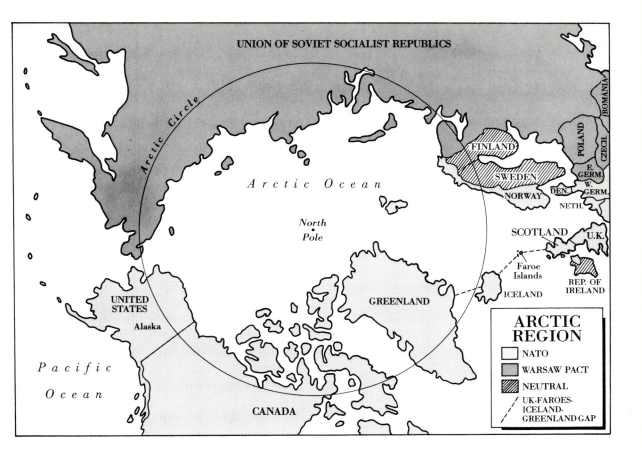

together under a series of unified commands, which would operate as one in the event of war.

Scotland has no separate voice within NATO. All decisions on foreign affairs and the defense of the U.K. are made in London. But as the northern part of an island sometimes dubbed "America's unsinkable aircraft carrier," Scotland hosts a large number of vital military installations.

One of Scotland's most important roles in the North Atlantic Treaty Organization (NATO) is as a link in a chain of islands straddling the main route for Soviet nuclear missile submarines trying to get from Russia's northern ports to the open Atlantic. The Shetland-Faroes-Iceland-Greenland gap is lined with top-secret listening devices. Royal

(in other words, British) Air Force antisubmarine aircraft fly endless search missions from their base in Lossiemouth, keeping tabs on the Soviet undersea fleet. A constant invisible war of electronic tricks and eavesdropping is carried out from bases such as the American-run Edzell. Royal Navy warships and submarines slip to and from their berths at Rosyth, a large naval base on the Firth of Forth.

More controversial is the heavy concentration of nuclear weapons in Scotland. There is said to be a higher proportion of nuclear weapons per head of population in Scotland than in any other country in the world. Not only does the Royal Navy site its nuclear missile submarines there, at Faslane on the Clyde, but the U.S. Navy has an important similar base at Holy Loch. A shroud of secrecy surrounds further installations, but there is thought to be at least one deeply buried stockpile of nuclear munitions elsewhere in Scotland.

Not surprisingly, such weapons provoke opposition from the people who have to live near them. Peace campaigners enjoy a lot of support in Scotland. But the strategic importance attached to Scotland by NATO planners makes it hard to imagine how England would ever allow it to leave the alliance and adopt a strategy of armed neutrality, as some have suggested. One of the conditions of any kind of future independence deal might be Scotland's acceptance of NATO membership, and of the existing military bases.

The Future Starts Here

Stretching out from teeming, congested Europe into the great expanses of the northern seas, Scotland is not in international terms any kind of

One of Britain's four Polaris submarines off the coast of Scotland. Based at Faslane on the Clyde, their American-made nuclear missiles are aimed at Russia; the finger on the button is that of the British Prime Minister. U.K. Ministry of Defence

waypoint or thoroughfare. It is, inevitably, a place of natives and emigrants rather than transients. There is no doubt many Scots enjoy this kind of end-of-the-road position, cherishing the unspoiled beauty of loch, mountain, island and shore with, perhaps, a trace of the smugness of the rat-race escapee. They know that behind the justified fears for the future of Gaelic, Scots dialects, Scottish customs, Scots law and an independent Scottish economy lies a hybrid, constantly changing but genuinely distinct Scottish culture: Scotland's sporting institutions, Scotland's food and drink, Scotland's architecture, an accent here, an attitude there.

The transport revolutions of the nineteenth and twentieth centuries have made Scotland far more accessible, but cannot change its position on the map. The increased ease of transportation of two particular items, however, does seem set to pose a major challenge to Scottish society over the next few decades, regardless of the actions of London, NATO or the EC.

First, tourists. Never before has it been so easy and so cheap for so many overseas visitors to come to Scotland. With enthusiastic support from government at national and local levels, ever more hotels, boarding houses and restaurants offer an ever-slicker range of packages tailor-made for any type of customer. Whether it's a couple from South Carolina seeking a weekend break to visit an ancestral birthplace on the Isle of Skye, or a Japanese businessman on a whirlwind golf tour, it can be arranged. To augment the innumerable historic ruins and fine buildings that stud the countryside, a sizeable "heritage industry" has grown up to mount exhibitions and build visitor centers demonstrating Scotland's vanished and vanishing lifestyles—a mining museum, for instance, where once there was a coal mine. This is all very well; it brings wealth to the country and is enjoyed by native Scots as much as by tourists. But with no apparent trailing off in the number of visitors,

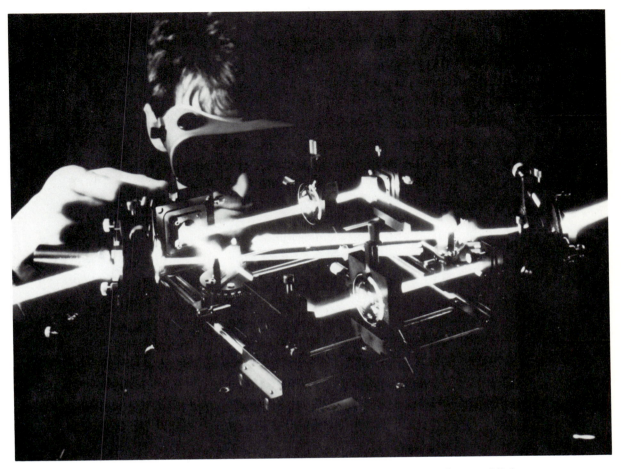

High-technology Scotland: the world's first digital circuit to operate on beams of light alone, developed at Scotland's Heriot-Watt University. It paves the way for the construction of optical computers, operating far faster than electronic ones. Heriot-Watt University

might the day not come when Scotland becomes a single gigantic theme park, a McDisneyland?

Second, information. The technology of the satellite, the silicon chip and the fiber-optic cable now renders geographical distance virtually irrelevant for certain companies involved in filing and processing large amounts of information. Accounts, financial transactions and reports can be transmitted from one computer to another, anywhere in the world, in a fraction of a second. Recently, British TV news carried a story about a New York insurance firm that found it was cheaper to set up a new data-processing center in Ireland than in the American city where its clients lived. An extreme case, perhaps; but an example of a phenomenon that will increasingly affect Scotland as a remote and congenial country already possessing good telecommunications links. If the long-predicted "global village" really is emerging, an outflow of jobs from the most congested parts of the developed world, such as west central Europe, to the least congested surely cannot be far away.

There is much to be hopeful about when crystal-ball gazing into Scotland's future, and it would be dangerous for the Scots to set their faces against changes that are inevitable. The lessons of the past are that Scotland's historic setbacks cannot be put down simply to foul play by the English, but are as much the result of the Scots' lack of foresight in anticipating change; and that no defeat, however depressing or shameful, is unsurvivable.

For the very fact that Scots continue to debate vigorously the future status of Scotland, and its powers of self-determination in matters political, economic, environmental and military, is proof enough that something of an independent nation lives on in their hearts and minds. The continuing attachment of the expatriate Scots to their homeland is further evidence. After all, they say, "You can take the man out of Scotland, but you can't take Scotland out of the man."

ABOUT THE AUTHOR

James Meek lives in Edinburgh, where he is a reporter for *The Scotsman*, a Scottish national daily newspaper. His assignments take him all over Scotland, from the Orkney Islands to the heart of Glasgow. He is coauthor of a play, *Faculty of Rats*, which was produced in Scotland, and has just published his first novel, *McFarlane Boils the Sea*.

Bibliography

While this book is as comprehensive and, the author hopes, as interesting as space allows, it cannot claim to present a complete picture of Scotland and Scottish life. A few of the ways readers can find out more about the land and its people are listed below.

The Land:
Natural history does not recognize political boundaries, and many informative books about Scottish wildlife cover a larger area than Scotland. One such is *The Living Isles: A Natural History of Britain & Ireland* (Peter Crawford, Scribner, 1987). Two interesting illustrated works covering the country's huge population of birds are *Birds in Scotland* (Valerie M. Thom, Buteo, 1986) and *Collins British Birds* (John Gooders, The Stephen Greene Press, 1982). One of the most enjoyable books ever written about Scottish wildlife is the world best-seller *Ring of Bright Water* (Gavin Maxwell, Penguin, 1965). An autobiographical story of a man bringing up otters in a remote cottage in the far northwest Highlands, it accurately conjures up the interplay of weather, sea, plants, fish, animals and birds that has been the annual cycle of the wilderness since the end of the Ice Age.

The People:

An excellent, highly readable starting point is the illustrated reference book *A Companion to Scottish Culture* (David Daiches, ed., Holmes and Meier, 1982). Its entries are written and laid out in a clear, straightforward way that is accessible to all but the youngest age groups—an ideal volume to leaf through and dip into at random. Good follow-ups would be *The Scots: A Portrait of the Scottish Soul at Home & Abroad* (Iain Finlayson, Atheneum, 1987) and, for a highly personal Scots-Canadian perspective with a strong historical slant, the illustrated *John Prebble's Scotland* (John Prebble, David and Charles, 1985).

Present-day travel guides to Scotland are common; modern travelogues about the country rare. But there is the intriguing *In the Footsteps of Johnson & Boswell: A Modern-Day Journey Through Scotland* (Israel Shenker, Oxford University Press, 1984; illustrated). The two gentlemen referred to, English wit and writer Dr. Samuel Johnson and his Scottish companion James Boswell, carried out a celebrated tour of the country in the eighteenth century. On language, there are a number of books with which people can learn Scots Gaelic, such as *Teach Yourself Gaelic* (Roderick Mackinnon, McKay, 1979). A sound introduction to Scots Gaelic culture is *The Companion to Gaelic Scotland* (Derick S. Thomson, Basil Blackwell, 1984; illustrated). Very few texts are available in the United States about modern Scots dialects and the old Scots tongue, but an indispensable aid to anyone embarking on a study of these areas is *The Concise Scots Dictionary: A Comprehensive One-Volume Dictionary of the Scots Language from the 12th Century to the Present Day* (M. Robinson, ed., Humanities Press International, 1985). Those interested in the fertile field of Scottish personal names should consult *Surnames of Scotland: Their Origin, Meaning & History* (George F. Black, New York Public Library, 1984).

Scotland's obsession with soccer is ably dealt with in *Scottish Football: A Pictorial History from 1867 to the Present Day* (Kevin McCarra, State Mutual Books, 1984).

There are a good number of books available dealing with food in Scotland. Among the best are *Modern Ways with Traditional Scottish Recipes* (Rosalie Gow, Gretna 1981) and *Scottish Fare* (Norma and Gordon Latimer, Latimers, 1987).

Readers wishing to delve more deeply into the issues of religion and education can turn to two volumes that are, however, likely to prove heavy going for younger readers: *The Social History of Religion in Modern Scotland* (Callum Brown, Routledge, Chapman and Hall, 1987) and *As Others See Us: Schooling & Social Mobility in Scotland & the United States* (Keith Hope, Cambridge University Press, 1985; illustrated).

History:

Frustratingly, a number of the best Scottish books, by such authors as T. C. Smout and John Prebble, are not in print in the United States. But there are plenty of sound, readable alternatives. *A Concise History of Scotland* (Fitzroy Maclean,

Thames and Hudson, 1983) is a richly illustrated book with a fast-paced narrative that makes it suitable for all ages. Other good general histories: *The History of Scotland* (Peter Fry and Fiona S. Fry, Routledge, 1985); *A History of Scotland* (J. D. Mackie, Penguin, 1984).

Scotland from the Earliest Times to 1603 (W. Croft Dickinson, Oxford University Press, 1977) deals with the period up to the Union of the Crowns. The country's more recent past is covered in *A Century of the Scottish People, 1830–1950* (T. C. Smout, Yale University Press, 1986) and *No Gods & Precious Few Heroes* (Christopher Harvie—on demand, reprint available from Division of University Microfilms International, 300 North Zeeb Road, Ann Arbor, MI). Many regularly occurring quibbles, queries and uncertainties can be settled by reference to *A Dictionary of Scottish History* (Gordon and John Donaldson, Humanities Press International, 1980).

An account of Scottish emigration to the United States can be found in *The Scotch-Irish Americans* (Peter Guttmacher, Chelsea House, 1988).

Art and Culture:

LITERATURE   Informative critical appraisals of Scotland's literature can be found in a number of volumes, such as *Introduction to Modern Scottish Literature* (Alan Bold, Longman's, 1983) and *Companion to Scottish Literature* (Trevor Royle, Gale Research Co., 1983).

Strangely, the superb James Hogg novel *Confessions of a Justified Sinner*, with which the reader of Scottish novels really ought to begin, appears to be out of print in the United States at present. Major municipal and academic libraries should have copies, however. Most of the other Scottish classics, by Sir Walter Scott and Robert Louis Stevenson, for example, are available in numerous editions. Other classics include *Sartor Resartus* (Thomas Carlyle, Everyman, 1967); *Annals of the Parish* (John Galt, Oxford University Press, 1986); *The House with the Green Shutters* (George D. Brown, Penguin, 1986); *A Scots Quair—Sunset Song, Cloud Howe, Grey Granite* (Lewis Grassic Gibbon, Schocken, 1982); *Magnus Merriman* (Eric Linklater, State Mutual Books, 1983); *Docherty* (William McIlvanney, State Mutual Books, 1980); *Lanark* (Alasdair Gray, Braziller, 1985); *Greyhound for Breakfast* (James Kelman, Farrar, Straus, 1987).

CHILDREN'S LITERATURE   Mollie Hunter has written many novels for young people about her native land, including: *Cat, Herself*; *The Haunted Mountain*; *Mermaid Summer*; *A Stranger Came Ashore*; *The Wicked One*; and *You Never Knew Her As I Did!*, a novel about Mary Stewart (all published by Harper & Row).

POETRY   Scotland's two most famous poets are available in a number of collections. For Robert Burns, one good edition is *Poems & Songs* (James Kingsley, ed., AMS

Press, 1969). For MacDiarmid, try *The Hugh MacDiarmid Anthology: Poems in Scots & English* (Hugh MacDiarmid, Routledge, 1972). He crops up again in one of the best introductions to twentieth-century Scottish poetry—*Seven Poets* (Hugh MacDiarmid, et al., Third Eye Centre, 1981). An excellent modern Scottish verse collection, beautifully presented and illustrated, is *Noise & Smoky Breath: An Illustrated Anthology of Glasgow Poems 1900–1983* (Hamish Whyte, ed., State Mutual Books, 1983).

ARCHITECTURE   A good introduction is *Buildings of Scotland* (Gifford & McWilliam, New York, Penguin, 1985). Also recommended is *Charles Rennie Mackintosh: Architect & Artist* (Robert MacLeod, Dutton, 1983).

MUSIC   *The Traditional and National Music of Scotland* (Francis Collinson, Routledge, 1972) is a fine introduction to its subject, combining meticulous research with a writing style that makes it suitable for all but the youngest readers. Other good texts are *Scotland in Music* (Roger Fiske, Cambridge University Press, 1972) and *The Emigrant Experience: Songs of Highland Emigrants in North America* (Margaret MacDonell, University of Toronto Press, 1982).

Scotland's Place Today: Chosen from a small initial pool, here are three books available in the United States that attempt to explain and/or challenge Scotland's curious political status. Each is written with college-level or higher audiences in mind. *Scotland: The Real Divide* (Gordon Brown and Robin Cook, eds., Humanities Press International, 1983); *In Bed with an Elephant: The Scottish Experience* (Paul H. Scott, State Mutual Books, 1986); *The Scottish Political System* (James G. Kelly, Cambridge University Press, 1985).

Discography

A wide variety of Scottish music is available on record, cassette or CD in the United States. *A Celebration of Scottish Music* is a compilation of Gaelic songs and Scots ballads, together with tunes on the fiddle, harp and bagpipe. It is available on the Flying Fish record label. Some other recordings: *Celtic Hotel* and *Music in Trust*, Volumes I and II, from the Battlefield Band, a modern folk group (Flying Fish); *Light on a Distant Shore* by Ossian, another folk group (Iona Records); *Coorse and Fine* (Springtyme Records), a selection of traditional songs from Dundee—a good example of the urban ballads of the nineteenth and twentieth centuries; there are also several with songs and instrumentals from the groups The Tannahill Weavers and Capercaillie (Green Linnet Records). Arrangements of many of Robert Burns's songs, performed by Jean Redpath, are available from Rounder Records. *Aite Mo Ghaoil*, by Christine Primrose (Flying Fish), and *Craobh Nan Ubhal*, by Flora MacNeil (Tangent Records), are recordings of Gaelic songs. Flying Fish has put out a number of bagpipe collections, including *Ceol Beg, Ceol Mor* by Iain MacFadyen and *A Controversy of Pipers*. For fiddle music there's *The Silver Bow* (Topic Records) and two records by Jim Johnstone & His Dance Band on Flying Fish: *Government Warning (This Record Will Make You Want to Dance)* and *Stramash*. Finally, for fans of the harp there are recordings by Sileas (Green Linnet Records) and a number of albums by Alison Kinnaird (Flying Fish).

Good record stores will stock albums by successful modern Scottish rock bands like Simple Minds, Big Country, Aztec Camera, Wet Wet Wet, The Proclaimers, Danny Wilson, Deacon Blue and Hue & Cry.

Filmography

A handful of Scottish movies have been made over the years. *Local Hero* is a recent comedy by the Scots director Bill Forsyth, about a Texan oil company and a small Highland fishing village who conspire to make millions from the development of an oil terminal. It is distributed by Warner Home Video. *Another Time, Another Place* is a poignant story set in a remote northeastern farming community in Scotland during the Second World War as a group of Italian prisoners of war arrives to help with the crops (Nelson Entertainment). Also set during the war, but filmed nearer the time, is *Whisky Galore.* It's a comedy about a Hebridean island where supplies of Scotch have run out . . . until a merchant vessel is reported wrecked offshore (HBO Home Video).

Grampian TV, the commercial TV station that broadcasts in the north of Scotland, has produced a special American-format video version of its acclaimed three-part documentary series about the Gaels, *The Blood Is Strong.* This is available from The Blood Is Strong, Network Scotland, PO Box 66, Inverness IV1 1GL, Scotland.

Several videos are available from the Scottish arm of the British Broadcasting Corporation. Episodes of the popular comedy series *Scotch and Wry*, starring Rikki Fulton, are available from BFS, 350 New Kirk Road, Richmond Hill, Ontario, Canada L4C 3G7. A video of the Edinburgh Military Tattoo, a display of Scottish martial pomp, pageantry and music, can be obtained from Public Media Inc., 5547 North Ravenswood Avenue, Chicago, IL 60640-1199.

Index

References to illustrations are in *italics*.

Picts, 29, 60–61, *92*, 93, 95–96

pipers, *211*, 212–13

place names, 28–30, 37

plaids, 152–54

poetry, 122, 187, 189–91, 194

Polaris submarine, *224*

police, 85

political conflicts, 59–62, 178–85, 216

political parties, 179, 181–85

political protests, *183*, *220*

population, x, 7–9, 46, 61, 66, 150, 174, 177, 198

porridge, 69–70, 150

potatoes, 47, 75–76, 160

Prime Minister, British, 179

Proclaimers, 210

produce, 47

Protestantism, 40, 62–63
    Reformation, 88, 127–36, 188

ptarmigan, *17*, 18

public services, 70, 176

pubs, 43, *44*

puffins, 25, *25*

Queen Mary, 167

railways, 70, 166–67

Ramsay, Allan, 207

Randolph, Thomas, 113

Rannoch Moor, 16

Reform Act, 180–81

regionalism, 59–62

religion, x, 40, 62–63, 97–98, 100
    Catholicism, 63, 97, 126–33
    conflicts, 141, 145–46
    Kirk, 62, 132–33, 143–46, 162, 178, 188

religion (*cont'd*)
    Protestant Reformation, 88, 127–36, 188

Renaissance, 121–24
    literary, twentieth century, 194

restaurants, 78

revolutions, 163–72

rivers, 20, *22*

roadways, 70, 172

Robert I (Robert Bruce). *See* Bruce, Robert

Robert II (Robert Stewart), King of Scotland, 118

Robertson, William, 168–70

Roman Catholicism, 63, 97, 126–33

Roman rule in Scotland, 88–93, *90*

romantic literature, 170–71, 172

Royal Council, 101

rugby, 82

Rutherford, Daniel, 171

St. Abb's Head, 10

St. Andrews, 81–82, 98

St. Andrew's Cross, 101

St. Andrews University, 75, 88, 122

salmon, 20–23

Saxons, 94

scenery. *See* landscapes

schiltrons, 108–9

schools, 47, 58, 63, 71–73, *72*

scientists, 170–71, 220

Scone, Pictish capital, 93

Scotch-Irish people, 141

scotch whisky, 49

Scotland, x–xi, 1–4, *8*
    government, 116–21
    languages, 30–37
    peoples, 29–30, 39–41, 44–45, 93–98